Vegan Seafood

Beyond the Fish Shtick
for Vegetarians

D0037272

Also by Chef Nancy Berkoff, RD

Vegan Menu for People with Diabetes

Vegan Microwave Cookbook

Vegan Passover Recipes

Vegan Meals for One or Two

Vegan in Volume

Vegan Seafood

Beyond the Fish Shtick
for Vegetarians

by Nancy Berkoff, EdD, RD, CCE

Nutrition Section
by Reed Mangels, PhD, RD

The Vegetarian Resource Group
Baltimore, Maryland

A Note to the Reader

The contents of *Vegan Seafood* and our other publications, including web information, are not intended to provide personal medical advice. Medical advice should be obtained from a qualified health professional. We often depend on product and ingredient information from company statements. It is impossible to be 100% sure about a statement, information can change, people have different views, and mistakes can be made. Please use your own best judgement about whether a product is suitable for you. To be sure, do further research or confirmation on your own.

© Copyright 2008, The Vegetarian Resource Group
PO Box 1463, Baltimore, MD 21203.

Cover artwork and illustrations by Keryl Cryer

Library of Congress Cataloging-in-Publication Data

Berkoff, Nancy.
  Vegan seafood : beyond the fish shtick for vegetarians /
by Nancy Berkoff ; nutrition section by Reed Mangels.
    p. cm.
Includes index.
  ISBN 978-0-931411-31-1
  1. Vegan cookery.
  I. Mangels, Reed.
  II. Title.
  TX837.B477628 2007
  641.5'636--dc22

                                    2007041803

Printed in the United States of America

10 9 8 7 6 5 4 3 2 1

Table of Contents

Dedication

SOME DEVOUT followers of the Hindu faith have told me that one earns karma points for purchasing a live fish from a fish market and releasing it back into the ocean or river. This book is dedicated to all those who increase their karma by using the following recipes, rather than captive or wild fish.

Acknowledgments

SPECIAL THANKS TO Reed Mangels, PhD, RD for contributing nutrition information to this book. Thanks to Susan Petrie and Charles Stahler for reviewing the entire manuscript and Andrew Ryan, RD, for completing the nutritional analyses for all the recipes. Finally, thanks to Keryl Cryer for designing the cover and doing the artwork and Debra Wasserman for coordinating all aspects of this book's production from start to finish, including the layout. Your help is greatly appreciated.

Introduction

SURELY IT'S POSSIBLE TO BE VEGAN AND STILL ENJOY THE TASTE OF THE SEA! Vegans who would like an animal-free "seafood" experience, have three options: purchasing "convenience" vegan products (such as vegan "tuna" or vegan "shrimp"), making original "seafood" creations, or approximate the ambiance of seafood menus (more about that later).

In this book we use three vegan "seafood" products and also offer suggestions for substitutes. Many recipes do not call for these items, so don't worry if you can't purchase these particular ingredients. They are:

> **Vegan "Tuna"**: when a chunky texture was appropriate, we used frozen vegan "tuna." This product may not have the look of real tuna, but it does have the taste. It can be mashed or chunked for use in cold salads and entrées, as well as hot soups, casseroles, and entrées. It can also be tossed with chopped raw vegetables and vegan mayonnaise for a fast salad or cut into vegetable chowder to transform it into "seafood" chowder. Vegan "tuna" can be combined with cooked pasta, frozen mixed vegetables, and your favorite soup to create a "tuna" bake.
>
> Thaw this substitute tuna in the refrigerator before you add it to menu items. Find vegan "tuna" frozen in some natural foods stores or order it (#C019) online at <www.vegieworld.com>.
>
> **Vegan "Fish" Fillet**: when a solid, more visible product is appropriate, you can use the recipe on page 48 or, if you are in southern California, you can purchase vegan "fish" fillets at Mother's Markets. Fillet-type vegan products can be used when you would like to dress up a solid product, such as a seitan "steak," and can be cooked whole, or cut into pieces or strips. For example, if you need a fast but elegant, entrée, you can bake a fillet after brushing it with olive oil and minced garlic. Serve it topped with chopped tomatoes and basil. You can add fillet strips to stir-frys or create a hot sandwich with a grilled fillet and thinly sliced grilled seasonal vegetables.

Vegan Shredded "Crab Meat": when a solid, chewier product is needed. This product is made by Asian producers and often contains wheat and yam starch, vegetable oil, paprika, water, sugar, and non-meat seasonings. We used this type of product if we wanted an ingredient that would retain its shape when tossed with cold ingredients or when cooked. Visit <www.vegecyber.com> for futher information.

Note: Other vegan seafood ingredients are available, and the products we chose are by no means the only ones to use.

Accept No Imitations

You will need to be an avid label reader when shopping for vegan "seafood" products. Proceed carefully when you see "mock" or "imitation" on labels. Some "mock/imitation" products are vegan or vegetarian (containing perhaps egg whites or whey).

But some "mock/imitation" products are shellfish substitutes, for people with allergies to lobster, shrimp, crab, and clams, etc. or to provide a lower cost alternative to shellfish. This type of "mock/imitation" product is usually made with mild-flavored fish or with soy and/or starchy vegetables injected with fish extract.

As always, proceed with caution when purchasing processed products, and you won't go wrong.

Finding Vegan "Seafood" Products

If you live in an area with Asian markets, you may be able to find mock seafood products. "Fish" fillets, "shrimp," "shredded crab and crab pieces," "tuna," "salmon," and "scallops" are often available. Natural food stores or supermarkets may stock vegan "seafood" products. Check out the freezer cases, but if you can't find vegan "seafood" products in your local markets, shop online at one of the sites listed on the next page.

www.vegieworld.com

May Wah Healthy Vegetarian Food, located at 213 Hester St. in New York City's Chinatown, offers Vege Fish, Tuna, Prawn, Shrimp Balls, and more. Read labels carefully to determine vegan items. Order online or visit their store.

www.vegecyber.com

This site sells Vege Crab Meat Shredded, Vege Crab Meat Balls, Vege Fish Ham, Vege King Prawn, Vege Salmon, and Vege Shrimp Balls.

www.veganessentials.com

This site sells Vegi-Scallops by Cedar Lake, Vege-Scallops by Vibrant Life, and Tuna(Not!) Salad Mix by Dixie Diner.

www.vegetarianstore.com

This online retailer sells canned Worthington Skallops, as well as Cedar Lake's Vegi-Scallops.

www.cedarlakefoods.com

This site offers canned Vegi-Scallops made from wheat/soy protein.

www.vegeking.com

Vegan Fish Steaks and Vegan Tuna Fillets that they distribute are sold at Mother's Markets in Southern California.

www.vegeusa.com

Offers Vegan Shrimp; however, you must call (888) 772-8343 to order this product.

www.veganstore.com

Pangea offers Cavi-art Vegan Caviar and Worthington Skallops.

www.worthingtonfoods.com

When you type in this address, you will probably find yourself in the Kellogg's site featuring Worthington Foods products. This company offers Vegetable Skallops made from textured vegetable protein.

What's in These Vegan "Seafood" Products?

The majority of the vegan "seafood" items we have seen are soy-based, with differing amounts of vegetable oil, water, artificial and natural flavors and colors, yeast, and flour (soy, corn, and others). Some "seafood" items are made primarily with yam flour. Most of the vegan "seafood" products we have found have been refrigerated, frozen, or canned.

Some vegan seafood products are made by large companies, such as Worthington Foods. Others are made in small neighborhood restaurant kitchens. Diversity in manufacturing means diversity in ingredients. In addition to soy and gluten, we have seen non-vegan ingredients, mostly milk solids and egg whites. Vegan ingredients include potatoes, carrots, taro, yam, celery, bell pepper, fresh and dried garlic, paprika, various vegetable oils, and yeast.

Since there is not a lot of uniformity in the manufacture of vegan "seafood" products, once again, be certain to read your labels. It was sometimes difficult to find vegetarian "seafood" products that did not contain sugar, in the form of maltodextrins, sucrose, dextrose, or corn syrup solids.

More Vegan "Seafood" Product Substitutes

Smoked Tofu: Smoked tofu makes a good substitute for smoked fish! Dice smoked tofu into small squares (about ½ inch x ½ inch) and toss with Italian-style salad dressing. Sauté and serve over pasta for a "smoked" seafood entrée. Diced smoked tofu can also be tossed with vegan mayonnaise and chopped onions and celery, seasoned with white pepper and used as a sandwich filling. Purée smoked tofu and mix with minced onions, bell peppers, black pepper, and red pepper flakes for a spicy "seafood" dip or spread. You can find smoked tofu in Asian and natural foods stores.

Dried Kelp Powder: Dried kelp seaweed powder mixed with a small amount of soy sauce approximates the taste of the ocean. Add to soups, such as potato chowder, to make a fast "seafood" chowder. Add to baked or grilled tofu, seitan, or tempeh for a fast "seafood" fillet. You can find dried kelp powder in Asian markets, some natural foods markets, and online.

Fish Sauce Susbstitute: If a recipe uses Asian fish sauce (it is either *nuoc mam* in Vietnamese or *nam pla* in Thai) you can usually replace it with half the amount of light soy sauce or Bragg Liquid Aminos along with a pinch of kelp powder for a "seafood" taste. Bragg Liquid Aminos is sold in natural foods stores or can be ordered online at <www.bragg.com>.

Dark Miso: Dark miso is a good substitute for anchovy paste or shrimp paste. Look for miso in natural foods stores or order it online at <www.healthy-eating.com>.

Nori: Nori, or dried seaweed sheets, come with a variety of seasonings, especially if you shop in Korean or Vietnamese markets. We've found various "heats" of chili, mushroom, and ground pepper used to season nori sheets. If you don't use the whole package of nori, wrap it so it is airtight, and store it in a cool, dry place (but not in the refrigerator or freezer, since it will become too moist).

Cooking with Vegan "Fish"

Non-seafood menu items can be quickly prepared with a variety of cooking techniques. Relying on the desired finished texture as a guide, match the vegan "seafood" product to its best cooking method. "Fish" fillet-type products lend themselves to moist heat cooking methods, such as poaching and steaming, or combination methods, such as broiling and grilling while basting (brushing or slowly dripping liquid over the cooking "fish").

"Shellfish"-type products, such as shrimp, lend themselves to both dry heat, such as baking or roasting, and moist heat cooking methods.

General "Fish" Preparation Guide

Grill: use "salmon"-type fillets and solid "fish" fillets. Marinate fish prior to grilling, and always brush with a small amount of vegan margarine or oil while cooking.

Bake or Roast: "fish" fillets and "salmon" can hold up to prolonged temperatures required for baking or roasting. You'll want to add a sauce, since the fish does not get a chance to caramelize in the oven. Season "fish" fillets with finely shredded fresh spinach and basil and minced garlic along with a small amount of cooking sherry, red wine, or vegetable juice cocktail (V-8 style) while they are cooking for an elegant entrée.

Sauté: the secret to successful sautéing is to cut "fish" into even pieces, and to cook over a fast heat. Try sautéed fish with red, yellow, and green pepper purée and black olives, or sautéed "salmon" with Moroccan preserved lemons and capers.

Steaming: steaming adds no fat to a dish, offering flavor with a seasoned liquid. There are many ways to steam "fish" fillets, including oven-steamed (called "en papillote") in parchment or foil. Steam Cantonese style with white wine or rice vinegar, green onions, ginger, garlic, sugar, and soy sauce.

Chemical Cooking: often offered in dishes called "ceviche" or "escabeche." In a ceviche, also spelled "seviche," the freshest seafood is "cooked" with acids from citrus juice and tomatoes. You can prepare a vegan ceviche for 6-8 hungry people by mixing ½ pound (8 ounces or 1 cup) of "shrimp" with 1/2 pound of "fish" fillets, and 2 ounces (about ¼ cup or 4 Tablespoons) of fresh lime juice. Cover, refrigerate, and allow to "cook" for 1 hour. After 1 hour, add 1 Table-spoon of chopped fresh chilies, 2 Tablespoons of chopped onions, 1 Tablespoon of chopped fresh cilantro, ½ cup of chopped tomatoes, 1 minced clove of garlic, and about 1 Tablespoon of olive oil. Chill and serve with crusty bread, a crisp green salad, and sparkling cider. Be certain to refrigerate any leftovers.

Smoking: smoking began as a food preservation method, but it's used nowadays more to add flavor than to extend shelflife. Vegan "fish" fillets are a bit lower in fat than most seafood, so brush them with a small amount of oil, or spray with vegetable oil before smoking. For stovetop smoking, place wood chips in a pan that can be placed on stove burners. Put a rack over the chips, add your "fish," cover, and put the stove burner on low. Allow "fish" to smoke until your product has absorbed a smoky flavor.

You can smoke portabello mushrooms, carrots, white and sweet potatoes, extra-firm tofu, seitan, and tempeh.

Seafood brines, to add additional flavor, can be combinations of salt (usually kosher or coarse salt), citrus juice, garlic, onions, and herbs or spices of your choice. Soak "fish" fillets for about 30 minutes prior to smoking, and/or brush on brine during smoking.

CAUTION: STOVETOP SMOKING REQUIRES LOTS OF VENTILATION, as in open windows and doors. A typical apartment-style hood is not enough ventilation. As with any type of indoor fire, carbon monoxide poisoning can result from inadequate ventilation. Some people invest in a small outdoor smoker.

Fish Trends

Classic seafood cooking techniques can be applied to vegan "seafood" products. Vegan "seafood," steamed, grilled, poached, or baked and served with colorful, flavorful accompaniments make wonderful meals.

Think international, as in "fish" fillets prepared by wrapping in aromatic leaves (such as banana or lotus) and steaming. You can find fresh leaves for steaming in Asian and Indian markets. Canned grape leaves are often available in the gourmet section of many markets. Wrap fillets in leaves, season with combinations of chopped garlic, onion, peppers, summer squash, tomatoes, fresh herbs (such as parsley, basil, sage, or oregano), and dried spices (such as white or black pepper, ginger, or red pepper flakes), and a dash of vegetable broth, tomato or carrot juice, and hot sauce and steam or bake until the flavors are combined.

Cha Ca, a Hanoi-style fish, is catfish marinated in ginger, chilies, fish sauce, and turmeric; stir-fried or sautéed with garlic, shallots, and dill; and served over rice noodles garnished with peanut granules. You can use vegan "fish" fillets to mimic this dish. For example, at Sencha, in Colorado Springs, Colorado, tuna-stuffed chile relleno with tequila mole includes diced fresh tuna and a mole flavored with garlic, onions, poblano chilies, tequila, chocolate syrup, cocoa powder, and five-spice powder. You can use vegan "tuna" or other vegan "fish" chunk products in place of the tuna for this dish.

Savory "Seafood" Dishes

Vegan "fish" tanjine with tomatoes and carrots is a Moroccan-inspired fish stew marinated with fresh parsley, fresh cilantro, olive oil, sweet paprika, saffron, and ginger. It's cooked with tomato concasse (tomato that has been peeled, seeds taken out, and then chopped finely), garlic, cumin, black pepper, carrot rondelles, and onions. Use vegan "fish" fillets as a substitute.

Indian-inspired vegan "shrimp" can be cooked in a tandoor, clay oven pot or oven-proof cast iron pot with coriander seed, cumin, black pepper, mustard seed, and fresh chili, served with a tomato, ginger, and almond sauce, and carrots tossed with fennel seed and mustard oil. Use vegan "shrimp" or other similar product.

A Taste of Tunisia uses shredded vegan "crab" or "tuna" mixed with parsley, cilantro, garlic, harissa (a fiery paste of pepper, chilies, garlic, ground coriander, and cayenne), a half-and-half mixture of silken tofu and soymilk (to help "glue" the ingredients), and breadcrumbs. This mixture is then formed into balls or croquettes and fried or baked and covered with a sauce made of tomato, olive oil, garlic, and vegetable broth with kelp powder. Serve over fine couscous.

"Cooked" sushi can be prepared with vegan "fish" fillets, quickly seared in a wok. Use olive oil for cooking fillets and season with chili powder, curry powder, sugar, and black pepper. Garnish with fresh cilantro before serving.

Finishing Touches

Many varieties of traditional seafood have a mild flavor. The sauce with which they are served is often what makes them a favorite dish. The following sauces can be served over baked, roasted or grilled "fish" fillets, mixed with vegan "tuna" and pasta or rice for casseroles, or used with hot dishes featuring vegan "shrimp" or "crab" products.

The sauces on this page yield approximately 2 cups or eight 2-ounce servings. These recipes can be halved successfully.

1. **Almond Sauce**: Prepare a paste with 2 Tablespoons of bread or all-purpose flour and 2 Tablespoons of vegan margarine. Gradually stir in ½ cup of soymilk and ½ cup of vegan sour cream. When thickened, remove from heat and stir in ½ cup toasted slivered almonds, 1 Tablespoon fresh lemon juice, and 3 Tablespoons chopped green onions.

2. **Shrimp-Oregano Sauce**: Chop 1 cup of vegan "shrimp" product. Melt 4 Tablespoons vegan margarine in a small sauce pot. Mince 3 garlic cloves and add to pot. Allow mixture to simmer for 5 minutes. Strain out garlic and discard garlic. Add chopped "shrimp," 2 teaspoons dried oregano, 1 teaspoon ground black pepper, and 4 ounces dry white wine (or substitute 1 Tablespoon apple juice, 2 Tablespoons white vinegar, and 2 Tablespoons water for the wine). Allow dish to simmer until flavors combine.

3. **Green Peppercorn Sauce**: Combine ½ cup softened vegan margarine, ¼ cup chopped fresh parsley, 1 Tablespoon pickled green peppercorns or capers, 2 teaspoons lemon juice, 1 teaspoon spicy prepared mustard, and ½ teaspoon soy sauce in a food processor or blender and process until smooth. Store in a glass or plastic container and refrigerate for at least 1 hour before serving. Scoop small servings onto sizzling hot vegan "fish" directly before serving.

4. **"Salmon" Dill Cream**: Combine 6 ounces vegan sour cream or unflavored soy yogurt with 5 Tablespoons chopped smoked tofu or vegan "salmon" product, 2 teaspoons chopped fresh dill, 1 teaspoon lemon juice, and 1 teaspoon finely minced sweet onion. Serve cold, with chilled or hot "fish" menu items.

"Sea Animals — Don't Eat Them!"

"Seafood" Stock

"Fish" stock can be made quickly and inexpensively. You just need a solid vegan "fish" product, such as "fish" fillets, chopped carrots, onions, and mushrooms, a little vegan margarine, a little wine or mild vinegar, some secret spices, a sturdy pot, and about 30-40 minutes. "Fish" stock holds for about 3 days in the refrigerator and for several months in the freezer.

"Fish" stocks, and their uptown cousins, fumets, are similar in flavor and can be used interchangeably. Both should be translucent liquids with a distinctive fish flavor. Fumet is a bit more acidic, using wine, brandy, or citrus juices to extract maximum flavor from the simmering ingredients. The perfect fish stock or fumet extracts flavors without over-concentrating them. Success is achieved by using a balance of "seafood" and seasoning.

To prepare a "fish" stock or fumet, select a thick-bottom pot or a steam kettle. Oil or vegan margarine is melted in the bottom of the pot. "Fish" and vegetables are sweated (cooked over low heat just until they begin to glisten, about 2-3 minutes, depending on the amount) to extract flavor, and then covered with water, wine, and a sachet (made of 4 fresh parsley stalks, chopped, 4 whole black pepper corns, and 1 teaspoon dried thyme), made from cheesecloth, a coffee filter, or a leek leaf. Allow stock/fumet to simmer until "seafood" aroma wafts over the stove. It should then be strained, cooled, and refrigerated or frozen until needed.

If you'd like to make a distinctive stock, you can add leeks and fennel, as well as tarragon to amplify the flavor. For a richer stock, add a small amount of tomato paste, white wine, and brandy when sweating the "seafood" and vegetables.

Lighter tasting fish stock takes about 30-40 minutes to prepare. Stronger stock takes approximately 40 minutes, ensuring that maximum flavor is extracted.

Court bouillon is not a stock, but is prepared using the same method. Court bouillon, although it sounds royal, stands for "short broth" in French. Court bouillon is actually a "poor man's" stock, because it contains no meat or fish. It is a flavored liquid, in which vegetables, vinegar and/or wine, and seasonings are simmered together to marry their flavors. Court bouillon is very widely used to poach fish and shellfish and perfect for vegan products as well.

For 1 gallon of court bouillon, combine 9 cups of water with ¾ cup of vinegar or dry white wine, ¼ cup of fresh lemon juice, 1 cup of chopped onions, ½ cup chopped carrots, ½ cup of chopped celery, 4 whole black peppercorns, 2 bay leaves, 1 teaspoon dried thyme, and about 10 fresh parsley stems (save the tops for garnishing). Bring all ingredients to a fast boil, reduce heat, and simmer for 45 minutes. Strain and cool until ready to use. Fortified bases can be prepared from ready-to-use bases with the addition of vegan "seafood," corncobs (for chowders), and other aromatic ingredients.

Court bouillon freezes well, so don't be afraid to fill a big pot. In addition to preparing "seafood" dishes, court bouillon can be used to steam or poach vegetables (such as broccoli or carrots), protein rich foods (such as extra firm-tofu or seitan), greens (such as spinach or kale), or as the cooking liquid for rice, pasta, quinoa, kasha, or whole wheat.

"Seafood" stocks can be used in a variety of menu items. Here are several ideas:

"Fish" Stews and Chowders: steam or boil potatoes and vegetables to be used in "fish" stews or stocks. This will enhance the flavor and ensure that the flavor is distributed evenly throughout the stew or chowder.

Hot Pots: prepare individual hot pots of savory "seafood" broths, made with "fish" stock, filled with vegan "scallops" and individual portions of vegan "fish" fillets. These can be presented steaming hot right to the table.

Rice and Pastas: use "fish" stock as part or all of the cooking liquid to prepare steamed rice, rice pilafs, and pastas to be served with "seafood" entrées.

Elegant Starter: season "fish" stocks or fumets with minced fresh herbs, such as basil, rosemary, thyme, or oregano and garnish with two or three pieces of vegan "shrimp" or "crab" for a light beginning to the meal.

When Vegan "Seafood" is Not an Option

Imagine the sounds and smells of the seaside! Chefs have been attempting to capture these sensations in a bowl or on a plate for centuries. You may have heard about some of the more successful dishes: Bourride with monkfish, saffron-scented Bouillabaisse, Chorizo (a dry Spanish sausage-flavored Paella), and Chaudiere (also known as "chowder") with lobster and clams.

But, you say, "How can a vegan enjoy these exotic Spanish, French, and Italian dishes? Their main ingredients are fish and seafood and I can't find any vegan seafood products in my area!" Here's a little secret: the success is not in the fish, but in the seasoning and the cooking style.

The seafood in these dishes are usually mild in flavor; they add a little character to the flavor, but not that much. What they do add is texture. There are many vegan ingredients that can be used in their place. Extra-firm tofu, smoked tofu, seitan, tempeh, potatoes, summer squash, and vegan sausage can lend their texture to seaside stews.

The cooking liquid is essential to develop the flavor of a "seafood" stew. As explained earlier, a court bouillon is used for poaching fish to add flavor and moisture. Visit any classical kitchen and you'll find a court bouillon simmering on the stove. You can use court bouillon to poach extra-firm tofu, plain or flavored seitan, plain or flavored tempeh, zucchini or summer squash, boiling potatoes, or mild flavored vegan meats, such as Tofurky™ or Field Roast™. We've included a recipe for a saffron broth (see page 30). You can use this fragrant liquid to add seaside flavor to vegetables and rice.

Provencale-style stews are French peasant-style stews with Italian and Spanish influences. To make anything "provencale," you need olive oil, onions, garlic, tomatoes, black pepper, and olives. Combine these ingredients and allow them to simmer. The combined flavors will give you the essence of a provencale fish stew without the fish. Add chunked eggplant, yellow squash, or potato, or extra-firm tofu or seitan pieces. Allow the dish to cook until you have incorporated the taste of the provencale vegetables, herbs, and spices.

Technique is important for developing flavor as well. For example Meuniere is a classic fish preparation, using lemon juice, parsley, butter, and lemon as garnish. The fish is cooked, coated in flour, seasoned with butter (you can substitute olive oil with a bit of nutritional yeast stirred in for flavor), salt and pepper, and served with a Meuniere garnish. You can prepare a nonseafood Meuniere with slices of extra-firm tofu, seitan "steak," thin slices of portabello mushrooms, or thinly sliced Russet potatoes.

A Sauce Portugaise is a traditional seafood sauce. French-style tomato sauce is made from tomato paste, onions, carrots, celery, parsley, peppercorns, and thyme and is allowed to simmer until thick. This sauce is combined with more tomatoes, onions, garlic, and parsley to make Sauce Portugaise. It is used to make fish stews and to serve over fish steaks. You can do the same with a summer squash and potato stew or seitan "steaks."

Oreganata is a classic way to prepare clams. Olive oil, onions, garlic, lemon juice, breadcrumbs, chopped parsley, oregano, white pepper, and paprika are used to make a thick paste. Clams are added, and the whole mixture is fried to make a hot appetizer. Instead of clams, you can use small cubes of cooked potatoes, mild vegan meats, or cubes of extra-firm or smoked tofu. If vegan "tuna" is available, you can use that as your "fish" ingredient. The ingredients and the spices overpower the flavor and texture of the clams. No one will ever guess that the Clams oreganata is clamless.

Much of the traditional flavor of seafood stews is from traditional herb blends used to make savory broths. Carrots, onions, and celery, known collectively as "mirepoix," are standard, as are bouquet garnis (sachets) of parsley stems, whole black peppercorns, ground thyme, and a small amount of garlic. Olive oil, leeks, and mushrooms, as well as white wine and lemon, complete the ingredients for a seaside flavor.

Let's move on to two main seasonings in the most well-known seaside stews, paella and bouillabaisse. Bay leaf, the deep green leaf of the sweet bay laurel, originated in the Mediterranean region. Ancient Greeks awarded bay laurel wreathes to outstanding scholars, renowned artists, and triumphant athletes. The word "baccalaureate" means "laurel berry" and was thought to have magical properties. Ancient Romans thought that bay leaves would protect them from the plague. In the Middle Ages, bay leaf was thought to bring good luck. The bay leaf is a powerful herb. It likes to simmer and marinate, developing slowly over time. Use bay leaf sparingly, as it can become very, very strong. It is better to use dried bay leaf, rather than fresh bay laurel leaves, since the fresh ones can have a harsh flavor. Store dried bay leaves in a cold, dry place in an airtight container. And purchase enough to make yourself a laurel wreath for perfecting the art of vegan "seafood" stews!

Called the "herb of the sun," saffron has been valued as a medicinal herb, a flavoring, perfume, and a dye for cloth. What makes saffron so expensive? Saffron is the dried stigmas of the crocus flower. The stigmas are the short, pollen-covered threads on the inside of the crocus. The crocus has a short, three-week blooming season once a year. Each crocus bulb produces only two to five flowers per harvest. The flowers have to be plucked from each flower by hand at the height of their bloom. Crocus flowers will yield for two years. After that time, the bulbs must be replaced.

It takes 2½ acres of land to produce 110 pounds of saffron crocus flowers. It takes 100,000 flowers to produce 11 pounds of fresh stigma, which dry to produce 2¼ pounds of dried saffron. To put it another way, you need 300,000 to 400,00 stigmas, about 75,000 to 85,000 flowers, to get just 1 pound of saffron.

But not to worry, you need very little saffron to flavor a menu item! One thread (one dried stigma), or as scientists like to put it, 1/547th of a pound, is enough to flavor a large pot of rice.

Saffron has been cultivated for a long time. It probably originated in Asia or Greece. We know it was a hot item for Phoenician traders and many other international vendors of the time. Murals in the palace of Knossos on Crete depict saffron harvesters and saffron is mentioned in the Song of Solomon. In the bible, ancient Greeks and Romans used saffron not just in food, but as a perfume and a dye. Of course, the Romans were lucky, since saffron grew wild in Italy at that time. The Middle East, Turkey, and India and its neighbors are modern saffron growers.

If you were in Istanbul, you could go to the Spice Market and haggle with the merchants over various grades of saffron. Always purchase saffron threads, not powder. The threads release more flavor and color and you can see the quality of what you are buying. Saffron powders can be of mixed quality and may have lost some of their coloring and flavoring ability.

Sometimes saffron containers have coloring strength listed. If the listed strength is less than 190 degrees of coloring strength, you might want to pass. Once you've selected your saffron, store it away from light and heat. Saffron easily absorbs other flavors, so segregate and keep it in an airtight container.

Allow yourself time to work with saffron. Saffron, if it's not "coaxed," loses both color and flavor. Since this spice is expensive, as well as delicate, it's worth an extra 15 minutes of preparation to extract all the color and flavor the threads have to offer.

If you are using whole threads, they should be soaked for at least 15 minutes. You can soak them up to 4 hours. The longer saffron soaks, the more the flavor develops. Some chefs soak and simmer saffron in milk and then add it to the liquids in the recipes. Or you can take some of the liquid from the recipe, bring it to a boil and stir saffron threads in. Remove this liquid from the heat and allow it to soak to bring out flavor and color.

If you find you prefer to work with powdered saffron, you should purchase threads and make your own powder. This guarantees you'll have high quality saffron. Toast saffron threads in a heated dry pan for about 1 minute to remove any moisture. You'll know you've toasted the saffron enough when the threads begin to give off a perfume. Cool and crush the threads finely and store in an airtight container.

You'll have to develop a taste for how much saffron to use. The general rule of thumb is about 1/8 teaspoon saffron threads per portion for soaked saffron. The recipes included in this book assume you are using soaked saffron threads.

Saffron: A Basic Guide

A small amount of saffron goes a long way, so be sure to follow amounts listed in recipes. Here is a general guide:

a. If using mostly for color, such as in sauce, ¼ teaspoon saffron threads soaked in 2 Tablespoons of hot water or rice milk will cover a recipe using 5-6 cups of flour.

b. If using for flavoring, ¼ teaspoon of saffron threads soaked in 2 Tablespoons of hot water or white wine will flavor 6-8 servings of soup, rice, or pasta.

There are two basic ways that saffron is prepared before being added as an ingredient; if possible, saffron threads should be used whole, not crushed.

1. For every teaspoon of saffron thread used, add 1 Tablespoon of water. Soak threads thoroughly. Add the saffron and soaking water to 2 ounces of additional water and allow to stand for at least 1 hour. Add to your saffron recipes.

2. If you must use saffron in a hurry, here is a fast, but less desirable way to prepare saffron. For every teaspoon of saffron, add 5 teaspoons of water. Soak the threads and press them firmly to the bottom of the container with the back of a spoon. This will form a pasty liquid. Add to your saffron recipes.

Additional Ideas for Using Saffron in Dishes

1. Cut carrots, potatoes, sweet onions, and zucchini into stew-size chunks. Poach in court bouillon and serve over saffron rice.

2. Fry tofu or seitan a la Meuniere and serve with a saffron mayonnaise (stir about 2 teaspoons of soaked and crumbled saffron threads into ¾ of a cup of vegan mayonnaise).

Vegan Seafood

If you don't have access to saffron, try these suggestions:

1. Marinate a combination of vegetables and vegan "meats" in a court bouillon with an added bay leaf for at least 3 hours. Roast until veggies are tender and serve with a parslied risotto.

2. If you'd like your soups and stews to taste a bit more "oceany" purchase fresh or dried seaweed. You can usually find sheets of dried seaweed in the specialty section of a large grocery store. Or you can cruise Asian markets for fresh or dried seaweed. Nori, the seaweed used as a wrapper for sushi, is a popular variety of seaweed. Add a very small amount to cooking liquid or court bouillon to give a briny, fresh taste to nonseafood dishes. The seaweed will add flavor and some color. Go easy with it until you find the balance of flavor you like. If you are using fresh seaweed, you will want to give it enough time to cook and soften. If you find fresh seaweed, you may want to prepare a side salad to serve with your seaside dishes. Cook and chill fresh seaweed and toss with a small amount of vinegar and red pepper flakes. Serve it cold.

3. If you don't have time to treat saffron or prepare special broth, here's an idea for a fast seaside stew. In a medium-size pot, combine 2 cans (about 8 ounces each) of chopped tomatoes, 1 large carrot, finely chopped (about ½ cup), and ¼ cup each finely chopped celery and onions. Add a bay leaf, cover, and allow mixture to simmer for 20 minutes or microwave on HIGH for 5 minutes. You now have the makings of a Provencale stew. Add ¼ cup sliced black olives, 1 teaspoon dried dill, and a sprinkle of garlic powder. You can spoon this over steamed potatoes or tofu for an aromatic entrée.

"Seafood" Suggestions with Vegan "Tuna"

(Note: if vegan "tuna" is not available, you may use smoked tofu instead.)

- To serve 4-6 people, defrost about 1½ cups of vegan "tuna" and chop. Mix with your favorite frozen mixed vegetables, cooked beans, and dry croutons. Use "fish" vegetable broth or vegetable juice to bind. Bake in a 400 degree oven for 10 minutes or until bubbly. Serve with a cool green or fruit salad.

- Combine chopped vegan "tuna" with diced green and red bell peppers, sweet onions, and chopped fresh tomatoes. Place on a slice of crusty bread, top with shredded vegan cheese, and bake or broil until cheese is bubbly.

- Create a Polynesian "tuna" salad with vegan sour cream, chopped pineapple, chopped celery, chopped green bell pepper, and a touch of shredded coconut.

- Create a vegan "tuna" Waldorf salad with vegan mayonnaise, chopped walnuts, apples, celery, and red grapes.

- Try a vegan "tuna" nicoise prepared with chopped black olives, diced, cooked potatoes, cut green beans, and an Italian-style vinaigrette.

"Seafood" Suggestions with Vegan Shredded "Crab" or "Shrimp" Products

(First, be sure to thaw "crab" or "shrimp" products in the refrigerator prior to use.)

- Add shredded "crab" or "shrimp" to hot vegetable broth and cooked noodles for a fast entrée.

- Create a "crab" or "shrimp" pasta salad by tossing shredded "crab" with minced celery and sweet onions, cooked and cooled rotini or spiral pasta, minced pimentos, minced fresh parsley, and vegan mayonnaise. For extra flavor, add a small amount of prepared horseradish, fresh lemon or lime juice, and tomato purée or hot sauce.

- Use shredded "crab" or "shrimp" to create sushi with nori, cooked and cooled short-grain rice, shredded cucumber, and thinly sliced avocado. For authentic flavor, toss the rice with a small amount of rice wine vinegar and sugar.

- Add shredded "crab" or "shrimp" to your favorite stir-fry.

- Create a baked vegan jambalaya by combining shredded "crab" and/or "shrimp" with cooked white rice, sliced okra, diced canned tomatoes, and minced celery, onions, garlic, and green bell pepper. For an authentic flavor, you may want to add some file (pronounced "feel-lay") powder (ground sassafras leaves) found in the spice section of your market.

- Add shredded "crab" to bean enchiladas to make a "crab" enchilada. (See recipe on page 63.)

- Use shredded "crab" or "shrimp" as a pizza topping.

Vegan "Fish" Recipes

Soups, Stocks, and Appetizers

BASIC "FISH" BROTH

Makes approximately 3 quarts or eight 12-ounce servings

2 pounds vegan "fish" fillets (double recipe on page 48 or use packaged vegan "fish" fillets)
3 quarts water (12 cups)
½ cup chopped onion
¼ cup chopped carrots
¼ cup chopped celery
½ cup chopped fresh mushrooms
2 dried bay leaves
1 teaspoon dried thyme
6 whole peppercorns
3 sprigs fresh parsley

Combine all ingredients in a small stockpot. Bring to a simmer, skimming as necessary to remove impurities. Allow broth to simmer for 30-40 minutes.

Strain, cool and store in refrigerator or freezer until ready to use.

Total calories per serving: 70
Total Fat as % of Daily Value: 3%
Protein: 8.6 g
Carbohydrates: 4 g
Iron: 1.6 mg

Dietary Fiber: 0.6 g
Fat: 2.3 g
Calcium: 43.8 mg
Sodium: 76.8 mg

SAFFRON BROTH WITH TOMATO AND "SEAFOOD"

Makes 5 eight-ounce servings

This delicate dish that showcases saffron's color and flavor is reminiscent of seaside cafes on the Mediterranean. Prepare it as close to serving time as possible.

I Tablespoon olive oil
½ cup chopped carrot
¼ cup chopped celery
¼ cup chopped onion
I cup chopped mushrooms
¼ cup chopped leek
2 cloves garlic, minced
½ cup frozen vegan "scallops" or "shrimp," not thawed
¼ cup dry white wine (or I Tablespoon white vinegar)
2 pinches saffron threads
I cup chopped plum (roma) tomatoes
I quart plus I cup mushroom stock or broth
10 or 12 small boiling potatoes, cooked
½ cup vegan shredded "crab" (optional)

Heat oil in a medium-size sauté pan. Add carrots, celery, onions, mushrooms, leek, and garlic. Sauté vegetables for 3 minutes, until they begin to sweat. Add vegan "scallops" or "shrimp," wine or vinegar, and tomatoes and sauté for 2 more minutes. Add stock, bring to a quick boil. Reduce heat and allow dish to simmer for 3 minutes. Strain the broth.

To serve, place two or three potatoes in each of the five soup bowls. If using "crab," divide evenly for each plate. Pour broth over potatoes and serve immediately (waiting diminishes the flavor of the saffron).

Total calories per serving: 450
Total Fat as % of Daily Value: 7%   Dietary Fiber: 12 g
Protein: 13 g   Fat: 5 g
Carbohydrates: 90 g   Calcium: 83 mg
Iron: 4 mg   Sodium: 1,025 mg

BASIC FUMET
(FLAVORFUL "FISH" BROTH)
Makes approximately 3 quarts or eight 12-ounce servings

4 Tablespoons vegetable oil
2 pounds vegan "fish" fillets (double recipe on page 48 or
    use packaged vegan "fish" fillets)
½ cup chopped carrots
½ cup chopped celery
1 cup chopped white or yellow onions
½ cup chopped mushrooms
3 quarts water (12 cups)
2 cups dry white wine (or ½ cup white vinegar)
6 sprigs parsley, chopped
1 Tablespoon whole black peppercorns
2 teaspoons salt
2 dried bay leaves

Heat oil in bottom of a medium-size pot. Place the "fish" fillets, carrots, celery, onions, and mushrooms in the pot and sweat (cook over low heat, just until vegetables begin to glisten) for approximately 3 minutes.

Cover with water and wine or vinegar. Add parsley, peppercorns, salt, and bay leaves. Allow broth to simmer for 30 minutes.

Strain stock; discard vegetables and seasonings.

Total calories per serving: 138
Total Fat as % of Daily Value: 14%   Dietary Fiber: 0.9 g
Protein: 9 g   Fat: 9 g
Carbohydrates: 5 g   Calcium: 47 mg
Iron: 1.6 mg   Sodium: 665 mg

RICH "SEAFOOD" BROTH

Makes 3 pints or approximately 8 servings

2½ pounds vegan "fish" fillets (double recipe on page 48 or use packaged vegan "fish" fillets)
2 teaspoons ground white pepper
6 cups mushroom broth or vegetable stock
½ cup finely minced carrots
½ cup finely minced shallots
2 teaspoons finely minced fresh ginger

Dice vegan "fish" fillets into small pieces. Refrigerate.

Combine remaining ingredients in a medium-size pot. Allow mixture to simmer until flavors are combined, about 30 minutes.

Add diced vegan "fish" fillets, and allow to poach in broth. Remove vegan "fish" and save to use in hot entrées, stir-frys, or cold salads. Strain broth and cool until ready to use.

Serving suggestions: Steam 4 servings of seasonal vegetables and 4 servings of cooked broad noodles. Place noodles in a soup plate or deep dinner plate. Arrange vegan "fish" and vegetables over noodles. Pour heated broth over vegan "fish" and serve immediately. Another option is to allow the vegan "fish" to cool. Toss with diced celery, onions, vegan mayonnaise, and nutritional yeast. Use as a sandwich filling or toss with bowtie or spiral pasta to create a cold salad.

Note: To poach in this recipe, add vegan "fish" into simmering broth; allow "fish" to cook in the broth until heated through, about 5-8 minutes, depending on the product used. When poached, "fish" should be cooked thoroughly enough to eat. Remove "fish" with a slotted spoon, to avoid losing liquid from the broth.

Total calories per serving: 131
Total Fat as % of Daily Value: 5%   Dietary Fiber: 1 g
Protein: 5 g   Fat: 3 g
Carbohydrates: 15 g   Calcium: 91 mg
Iron: 2.4 mg   Sodium: 194 mg

CREAMY SMOKED "FISH" SOUP STARTER

Makes approximately 4 cups

Use this mixture as your starter liquid for "seafood" chowders, "fish" stews, casseroles, or pasta sauces.

2 Tablespoons vegetable oil
2 cloves garlic, minced
1½ cups minced onions
1 cup peeled and diced baking potato
½ cup finely diced carrot
1 pound diced smoked tofu (16 ounces)
3 Tablespoons chopped fresh parsley
1 bay leaf
¾ cup tomato purée
3½ cups water
¾ cup vegan sour cream
2 teaspoons ground black pepper
¼ teaspoon ground nutmeg

Heat oil in the bottom of a 2-quart pot. Sweat garlic and onions until they glisten, about 2 minutes. Add potatoes and carrots, stir and cook for 5 minutes or just until carrots begin to soften.

Add smoked tofu, parsley, bay leaf, tomato purée, and water. Allow to simmer for 30 minutes or until vegetables are tender.

Whisk in vegan sour cream, pepper, and nutmeg and allow to simmer for 5 minutes longer or until hot.

Notes: If you like, you may use diced vegan "fish" fillets (recipe on page 48) instead of smoked tofu. Use this basic soup to create corn and smoked "fish" chowder or winter squash, potato, and smoked "fish" chowder.

Total calories per 1 cup serving: 334
Total Fat as % of Daily Value: 26%
Protein: 13 g
Carbohydrates: 35 g
Iron: 3 mg

Dietary Fiber: 3.8 g
Fat: 17 g
Calcium: 78 mg
Sodium: 515 mg

OCEAN AND SEA MINESTRONE
Makes 1 quart or about 5 servings

1 cup vegan "shrimp" (or mixed vegan "shrimp" and "crab")
2 Tablespoons dry white wine (or 1 Tablespoon white vinegar)
4 cups "fish" stock or fumet (see page 31)
2 diced vegan "bacon" strips (about 1 Tablespoon)
1 Tablespoon olive oil
½ cup minced shallots or onions
¼ cup minced celery
2 cloves garlic, minced
3 Tablespoons tomato paste
1 cup fresh tomato concasse (peeled, diced fresh tomatoes)
4 Tablespoons uncooked short grain rice
1¼ cups cooked white beans
1 bay leaf
1 teaspoon dried chopped thyme
½ teaspoon dried rosemary

Steam the "shrimp" or "seafood" mixture in the wine or vinegar (this can happen in the microwave by placing ingredients in a covered bowl and microwaving on HIGH for 1½ minutes). Drain and add wine or vinegar to stock or fumet. Chop and refrigerate "seafood" until needed.

Place stock or fumet in medium-size pot and allow to simmer. Place chopped bacon strips and olive oil in a small frying pan. Sweat along with shallots, celery, and garlic only until they glisten, about 2 minutes. Add tomato paste and allow to brown.

Add tomato paste mixture and tomato concasse to fumet and stir to combine. Allow to simmer for 5 minutes. Add rice, beans, and herbs and allow to simmer until rice is cooked, about 20 minutes. Stir in "shrimp" or "seafood." Simmer for 5 minutes. Serve hot.

Total calories per serving: 251
Total Fat as % of Daily Value: 15%
Protein: 11 g
Carbohydrates: 30 g
Iron: 4 mg

Dietary Fiber: 5 g
Fat: 10 g
Calcium: 92 mg
Sodium: 686 mg

MANHATTAN-STYLE CHOWDER

Serves 5

Vegetable oil spray
1 cup diced onion
½ cup diced carrots
1 clove garlic, minced
¼ cup diced red bell pepper
3 cups "fish" broth or fumet (see recipes on pages 29 and 31)
3 cups canned diced tomatoes (not drained)
1 cup peeled, diced red or white wax potatoes
½ cup diced celery
1 cup cut corn (thawed if frozen, fresh if off the cob, drained if canned)
1 cup chunked vegan "tuna" (defrosted in refrigerator)
½ cup crumbled seaweed (such as nori)
¼ cup chopped fresh parsley
1 bay leaf
½ teaspoon dried thyme
1 teaspoon ground black pepper
1 Tablespoon soy bacon bits

Spray a large pot with oil and heat. Add onions, carrots, garlic, and red pepper and sauté for 2 minutes. Add all remaining ingredients. Bring to a fast boil, reduce heat, cover, and simmer for 20 minutes before serving.

Total calories per serving: 202
Total Fat as % of Daily Value: 9%
Protein: 11 g
Carbohydrates: 30 g
Iron: 4 mg

Dietary Fiber: 6 g
Fat: 6 g
Calcium: 114 mg
Sodium: 642 mg

EGGPLANT CAVIAR

Makes about 2 cups or eight ¼ cup servings

1 pound eggplant
2 teaspoons olive oil
½ cup sliced fresh mushrooms
⅓ cup chopped, seeded green bell pepper
⅓ cup sliced green onion (white section only)
1 clove garlic, minced
3 Tablespoons diced black olives
1 Tablespoon fresh lemon juice
1 teaspoon ground black pepper
2 teaspoons kelp powder or ground dried nori (optional)
2 Tablespoons chopped pine nuts or almonds (optional)

Preheat oven to 425 degrees. Using a fork, prick the skin of the eggplant in several spots. Place the eggplant on a non-stick cookie sheet and bake for 35-40 minutes or until soft and starting to collapse. Remove from oven and set aside to cool.

Put olive oil in a skillet and sauté the mushrooms and green peppers for 3 minutes. Add the green onion and garlic and sauté an additional 3-5 minutes or until the vegetables are tender. Allow vegetables to cool for 5 minutes.

Carefully remove the stem from the eggplant. Cut the eggplant in half lengthwise. Using a spoon, scrape the soft interior of the eggplant into a food processor or blender canister. The peel can be discarded. Add the sautéed vegetables, olives, lemon juice, pepper, and kelp or nori powder and blend until smooth.

Place in a bowl and allow caviar to chill for at least 2 hours before serving. Garnish with nuts, if desired.

Total calories per serving: 41
Total Fat as % of Daily Value: 3%   Dietary Fiber: 3 g
Protein: 1 g   Fat: 2 g
Carbohydrates: 6 g   Calcium: 15 mg
Iron: 0.5 mg   Sodium: 33 mg

VEGAN GEFILTE "FISH"
Serves 5

It takes some planning to assemble this dish, since the nuts need to soak for at least 6 hours before preparing the recipe.

- ½ cup whole unroasted cashews (pre-soaked)
- ½ cup whole unroasted almonds (pre-soaked)
- ½ cup whole pine nuts (pre-soaked)
- 2 cloves garlic, minced
- ¼ cup lemon juice (a bit more can be used, if a lot of "tang" is desired)
- I cup cold vegetable broth (entire amount may not be needed)
- ½ cup finely minced green onions (both white and green)
- ¼ cup minced parsley
- ¼ cup minced fresh dill
- I Tablespoon ground dried nori or kelp powder
- I Tablespoon Braggs Liquid Aminos or soy sauce

Place the cashews, almonds, pine nuts, and garlic in the canister of a food processor. Process mixture until very smooth; then place mixture into a bowl. Add lemon juice and mix to combine. Add just enough vegetable broth to create a paste that can be molded into shape. Add onions, parsley, dill, nori or kelp powder, and Braggs Liquid Aminos. Form into balls or patties, as desired. Cover and refrigerate for at least 3 hours.

Serve on a bed of lettuce and garnish with grated horseradish, if desired.

Note: If you can't find ground nori or kelp powder, you can purchase sushi wrappers, which are sheets of dried nori. Grind the nori sheets by hand, or in a spice grinder. The nori or kelp helps to impart a "fish" flavor. If you cannot find either one, mix in approximately 2 Tablespoons of prepared (jarred) horseradish, which will impart a traditional flavor.

Total calories per serving: 294
Total Fat as % of Daily Value: 36%
Protein: 9 g
Carbohydrates: 17 g
Iron: 3.1 mg

Dietary Fiber: 3 g
Fat: 23 g
Calcium: 66 mg
Sodium: 460 mg

Salads

VEGAN "TUNA" SALAD
Serves 6

Serve as a sandwich filling or as part of an entrée salad. You can also form this mixture into patties and bake for a tuna croquette entrée.

- 1 ½ cups crumbled vegan "tuna" or crumbled smoked tofu
- ½ cup vegan mayonnaise
- ¼ cup minced celery
- ¼ cup minced sweet onions (such as Maui or Vidalia)
- 2 Tablespoons minced dill pickle
- ½ teaspoon ground white pepper

Place all ingredients in a bowl and mix to combine. Cover and chill for at least 2 hours before serving.

Note: To transform this salad into croquettes or patties, you may add a bit of soft silken tofu and some dry breadcrumbs for a firmer texture.

Total calories per serving: 109
Total Fat as % of Daily Value: 12%
Protein: 7 g
Carbohydrates: 3 g
Iron: 1 mg

Dietary Fiber: 0.5 g
Fat: 7 g
Calcium: 37 mg
Sodium: 312 mg

MANGO SALAD WITH AVOCADO AND "SHRIMP"

Serves 4 entrées or 6 appetizer portions

2 heads Romaine lettuce
I cup vegan "shrimp"
I Tablespoon olive oil
I teaspoon white pepper
I cup diced fresh mango
2 Tablespoons fresh lime juice
½ cup diced avocado
3 Tablespoons rice wine vinegar
I teaspoon grated fresh ginger
½ teaspoon chopped fresh chili
½ cup olive oil
I teaspoon chopped fresh basil

Coarsely chop Romaine lettuce and arrange on a serving platter.

Heat a small sauté pan and add 1 Tablespoon olive oil. Sauté vegan "shrimp" along with white pepper until thoroughly heated. Set aside.

Toss mango, lime juice, and avocado together and arrange on Romaine lettuce.

In a small bowl, mix vinegar, ginger, chili, ½ cup oil, and basil to combine. Arrange "shrimp" over mango. Dress with vinegar mixture and serve immediately.

Note: Beware, this recipe is high in fat.

Total calories per entrée serving: 458
Total Fat as % of Daily Value: 55%   Dietary Fiber: 10 g
Protein: 6 g   Fat: 36 g
Carbohydrates: 35 g   Calcium: 465 mg
Iron: 4.5 mg   Sodium: 1,030 mg

WHERE'S THE SEAFOOD? SALAD
Serves 6

1 ½ cups raw peeled and grated parsnips
3 Tablespoons lemon juice
1 cup sliced celery
½ cup chopped walnuts
1 cup diced smoked tofu
¼ cup chopped sweet onions
1 teaspoon white pepper
Approximately ½ cup vegan mayonnaise

Place grated parsnip in a large bowl. If necessary, squeeze out any liquid.

Toss the parsnip with lemon juice. Add the celery, walnuts, tofu, onion, and pepper and toss gently to combine. Add the mayonnaise gradually, using just enough to moisten the ingredients.

Chill at least 30 minutes before serving.

Note: Defrosted, chopped vegan "tuna" may be used in place of smoked tofu.

Total calories per serving: 193
Total Fat as % of Daily Value: 21%   Dietary Fiber: 3 g
Protein: 9 g   Fat: 14 g
Carbohydrates: 11 g   Calcium: 56 mg
Iron: 1.4 mg   Sodium: 208 mg

Note: Instructions on how to prepare other salads including a Polynesian salad, waldorf salad, and "crab" or "shrimp" pasta salad can be found on pages 26-27.

Vegan Seafood

Main Dishes

SAFFRON RICE AND VEGETABLE STEW WITHOUT "SEAFOOD"

Serves 10

A paella pan is as wide and thick as a Dutch oven, but has low sides. If you don't have a paella pan, use a heavy soup pot or Dutch oven.

¼ cup olive oil
3 cups chopped onions
1 cup green bell pepper, seeded and cut into thin strips
1 cup red bell pepper, seeded and cut into thin strips
4 cups short-grain rice
1 quart (4 cups) vegetable stock or broth
1 teaspoon saffron threads, soaked in 1 cup boiling water
3 cloves garlic, crushed
2 cups cubed extra-firm tofu or smoked tofu
2 cups cubed smoked seitan or Tofurky™
2 cups Soyrizo™ or sliced vegan sausage
2 cups cubed zucchini
2 cups frozen, thawed green peas

Place oil in large sauté pan and heat. Add onions and peppers and sauté until tender, about 4 minutes. Add rice and stir until grains are coated and transparent and the oil is absorbed. Add stock, saffron, garlic, and stir. Add, placing in layers, the tofu, seitan or Tofurky™, Soyrizo™ or vegan sausage, zucchini, and peas. Bring to a fast boil. Lower heat, cover and simmer, stirring occasionally, until all the liquid is absorbed and rice is tender, about 30 minutes. Keep warm until ready to serve.

Total calories per serving (using seitan and vegan sausage): 617
Total Fat as % of Daily Value: 18%

Protein: 41 g	Dietary Fiber: 6 g
Carbohydrates: 87 g	Fat: 12 g
Iron: 7.6 mg	Calcium: 110 mg
	Sodium: 585 mg

ORZO PILAF WITH SUN-DRIED TOMATOES, SAFFRON, AND "CRAB"

Makes 8 four-ounce servings

Serve as an entrée, paired with a lettuce, grape, and walnut salad.

4 Tablespoons sun-dried tomatoes cut into thin strips
1 cup orzo pasta
Vegetable oil spray
2 cloves garlic, minced
6 Tablespoons minced red onion
½ cup dry white wine or vegetable broth
1 teaspoon olive oil
¼ teaspoon saffron threads
2 ounces shredded fresh basil
4 Tablespoons (2 ounces) shredded vegan "crab"

Place sun-dried tomatoes in a small bowl and cover with water. Set aside.

Bring 2 cups of water to boil. Add orzo and cook until al dente (still chewy). Drain and set aside.

Spray a small sauté pan with oil. Add garlic and onions and sauté for 2 minutes.

Combine wine or broth, oil, and saffron in a small pot and bring to a quick boil. Remove from heat and set aside. A little at a time, add orzo to garlic and onions, stir and continue to heat. Add tomatoes and stir. Add orzo and half the saffron liquid. Stir. Add remaining orzo and saffron liquid and stir until heated thoroughly and most of the liquid has been absorbed. Keep warm.

Right before serving, divide basil and vegan "crab" into individual bowls. Pour orzo over basil and vegan "crab" and serve.

Total calories per serving: 120
Total Fat as % of Daily Value: 2%   Dietary Fiber: 2 g
Protein: 21 g   Fat: 1 g
Carbohydrates: 21 g   Calcium: 21.8 mg
Iron: 0.7 mg   Sodium: 39 mg

Vegan Seafood

BOUILLABAISSE VEGAN (OR NON-FISHERMAN'S) STEW
Serves 10

Everyone will want to take a walk on the beach after this meal.

½ cup olive oil
1 cup sliced onions
1 cup julienned leeks
2 cloves garlic, minced
½ teaspoon fennel seed
1½ cups canned chopped tomatoes, drained
4 cups vegetable stock
½ cup white wine
2 bay leaves
2 Tablespoons fresh chopped parsley
½ teaspoon thyme
1 teaspoon cracked black pepper
1½ pounds (3½ cups) extra-firm tofu, drained and cubed
1 pound (2¼ cups) smoked vegan meat, such as seitan,
  Field Roast™, or Tofurky,™ cubed
1 pound (2½ cups) zucchini or yellow summer squash,
  cubed
1 pound (2½ cups) fresh button mushroom caps

Place oil in a heavy soup pot or Dutch oven. Heat and add onions, leeks, garlic, and fennel seed. Allow mixture to cook, stirring, until softened, about 4 minutes.

Add remaining ingredients and bring to a fast boil. Reduce heat, cover, and allow stew to simmer until the squash is tender, about 15 minutes. Serve hot, with rice or couscous.

Total calories per serving: 370
Total Fat as % of Daily Value: 22%   Dietary Fiber: 2 g
Protein: 41 g   Fat: 14 g
Carbohydrates: 20 g   Calcium: 124 mg
Iron: 4.5 mg   Sodium: 479 mg

BASIC BATTERED "FISH" WITH "FISH" SAUCE
Serves 6

6-8 half-inch thick slices of smoked tofu
1 cup all-purpose flour or unbleached flour combined well
with 1 Tablespoon baking soda
12-ounce can alcoholic or nonalcoholic beer (about
1¼ cups)
2 teaspoons ground black pepper
1 teaspoon paprika
1 cup all-purpose flour or unbleached flour (if needed)
Vegetable oil or vegetable oil spray

Place smoked tofu in a colander and put weight on top. Drain tofu for at least 2 hours and then pat dry. Set aside.

Mix batter ingredients together in a bowl. Dip slices of smoked tofu in the flour until lightly coated, then dip in batter. You can deep-fry in oil until golden brown, about 2 minutes or preheat an oven to 400 degrees, spray a baking sheet with oil, and bake breaded fillets until crispy.

Notes: Additional flour may be needed if a thicker breading is desired. This recipe also will work with sliced vegan "shrimp" for a seafood dish. Sliced, partially cooked white potatoes can also be battered and fried. If you prefer not to use beer, use 1¼ cups sparkling water or seltzer mixed with 2 teaspoons of malt powder or nutritional yeast.

Total calories per serving (baked): 157
Total Fat as % of Daily Value: 4%   Dietary Fiber: 1 g
Protein: 11 g   Fat: 2 g
Carbohydrates: 20 g   Calcium: 44 mg
Iron: 2.6 mg   Sodium: 689 mg

VEGETARIAN "FISH" SAUCE

Makes approximately 3 cups or twenty-four $^1/8$ cup servings

This is a vegan version of a traditional Asian fish sauce.

1 ½ cups shredded dried seaweed
4 cups water
3 cloves garlic, minced
2 Tablespoons whole peppercorns
½ cup soy sauce
Water, as needed

Place the seaweed in a pot and add water. Bring to a fast boil, immediately turn down heat to a lower boil (still seeing lots of bubbles). Cook for 20 minutes.

Add the rest of the ingredients and enough water to make about 6 cups total in the pot. Bring back to a boil, then simmer for an additional 30-40 minutes.

When the sauce is reduced by about half (about 3 cups), it will taste almost too salty to eat; that means it is ready! Strain sauce through a fine sieve or coffee filter (be certain to remove all the peppercorns). Cool for at least 1 hour. Serve cold, with battered "fish" fillets.

Total calories per serving: 48
Total Fat as % of Daily Value: 1%   Dietary Fiber: 1 g
Protein: 1 g   Fat: 1 g
Carbohydrates: 12 g   Calcium: 92 mg
Iron: 3.3 mg   Sodium: 275 mg

TOFU "FISH" STICKS (FRIED)

Makes about 10 fish sticks or 2 servings

Depending on your diners, you may want to purchase cookie cutters in various shapes and cut out the tofu before breading.

I block extra-firm tofu (about I pound)
2 Tablespoons vinegar
I cup dry breadcrumbs
I cup panko (rice cracker crumbs)
2 cups oil for frying (approximately)
Potato chips and cooked green peas (optional)

Press tofu gently with your palm to extract any fluid. Place in a bowl, sprinkle with vinegar, cover with plastic or waxed paper, and weigh down with several heavy plates for 1 hour.

Cut tofu into 10 long strips, French-fry shaped. Pour oil into a large pot and heat. Mix bread and panko crumbs together. Place in a bowl. Dredge each tofu strip through the crumbs to thoroughly coat. Fry each tofu stick until coating is crispy. Pat additional oil from each stick with paper towels.

Arrange on a serving plate and garnish with potato chips and peas (a traditional English garnish).

Note: This recipe is very high in fat. The next page offers a "fish" stick that is lower in fat. Also, if panko is not available, you may substitute matzoh meal. The matzoh is a bit heavier, but will work. This recipe does not work well when oven-fried.

Total calories per serving: 1,279
Total Fat as % of Daily Value: 116%   Dietary Fiber: 7 g
Protein: 37 g   Fat: 75 g
Carbohydrates: 125 g   Calcium: 509 mg
Iron: 8.3 mg   Sodium: 486 mg

BAKED "FISH" STICKS
Makes about 10 sticks or 2 servings

Serve this with baked potato wedges for a healthy version of "fish" and chips.

1 block extra-firm tofu (about 1 pound)
⅔ cup cornmeal
2 teaspoons paprika
2 teaspoons kelp powder or ground nori
1 teaspoon onion powder
1 teaspoon garlic powder
1 teaspoon white pepper
½ cup soymilk
3 Tablespoons lemon juice
Vegetable oil spray

Preheat oven to 400 degrees. Drain tofu and set aside. Combine cornmeal paprika, kelp powder, and onion and garlic powder in a large bowl. Set aside. Pour soymilk into a large bowl. Set aside. Cut tofu into French-fry sized sticks.

Spray a baking sheet with oil. Set aside. Dip each tofu stick into soymilk, drain, and then dredge in cornmeal. Place on baking sheet. Repeat until all sticks are coated.

Spray coated sticks lightly with oil. Place in oven and bake 10-15 minutes or until crispy. Place on serving platter, sprinkle with lemon juice, and serve hot.

Total calories per serving: 409
Total Fat as % of Daily Value: 25%   Dietary Fiber: 6 g
Protein: 30 g   Fat: 16 g
Carbohydrates: 45 g   Calcium: 442 mg
Iron: 7 mg   Sodium: 74 mg

VEGAN "FISH" FILLETS

Makes about 8 fillets (each fillet is about 2 ounces)

**1 pound medium-firm or silken tofu, cut into 8 equally-
sized slices**
1 cup cold water
2 Tablespoons lemon juice
4 Tablespoons nutritional yeast
2 teaspoons dried kelp powder or ground nori
1 teaspoon dried parsley
**2 cups smashed cornflakes, crisped rice, or plain
(unsweetened) cold cereal of your choice**
1 cup whole wheat flour or all-purpose flour
Vegetable oil spray

Place tofu slices separately on a large plate. Set aside. In a shallow bowl
(you'll be placing the tofu in it) whisk together water, lemon juice, nutritional yeast, kelp or nori powder, and parsley. Gently arrange tofu in a
single layer in this dish. Let marinate in the refrigerator for at least 3 hours
or overnight. Turn at least twice.

Preheat oven to 450 degrees. Spray a cookie sheet with oil. To assemble
your fillets, pour smashed cereal onto one dinner plate and the flour onto
another plate. If there is any liquid left with the tofu, drain, and discard.
Gently dredge each piece of tofu first in the flour, then in the cereal,
brushing off any excess crumbs (avoid a thick coating). Place each coated
tofu piece on the cookie sheet. Place sheet in oven and bake for 5 minutes
or until just turning golden, turning once.

Remove from oven and place on serving dish. Serve hot, or store fillets
covered in the refrigerator until ready to serve.

Total calories per serving: 139
Total Fat as % of Daily Value: 3%   Dietary Fiber: 3 g
Protein: 11 g   Fat: 2 g
Carbohydrates: 21 g   Calcium: 36 mg
Iron: 3.1 mg   Sodium: 123 mg

FAST ARROZ ESPAGNOLE WITH "SHRIMP"

Serves 6

This dish is perfect for leftover rice.

- **1 cup vegan "shrimp" or smoked tofu**
- **4 cups cooked white or brown rice (begin with 2 cups uncooked rice)**
- **1¾ cups prepared tomato sauce**
- **½ cup salsa**
- **½ cup canned or cooked, drained black beans**

If necessary, cut up vegan "shrimp" into bite-size pieces. Set aside.

Place cooked rice in a large pot. Stir in sauce, salsa, and beans and reheat, covered, over low heat for 5 minutes. Stir in "shrimp." Cook an additional 10 minutes or until mixture is thoroughly hot. Serve.

Total calories per serving (using tofu and brown rice): 233
Total Fat as % of Daily Value: 6%	Dietary Fiber: 5 g
Protein: 10 g	Fat: 4 g
Carbohydrates: 42 g	Calcium: 98 mg
Iron: 2.2 mg	Sodium: 507 mg

MAKE YOUR OWN "SEAFOOD" (ASIAN-FLAVORED SEITAN)

Makes approximately 1½ pounds cooked seitan or 4 servings

Seitan "seafood" can be used in stir-fries, casseroles, and baked entrées. Add some nori or kelp powder to the cooking liquid for a more intense seafood taste. Purchase uncooked seitan (gluten) in the refrigerator or freezer section of Asian markets and natural food stores. Store the seitan in the cooking liquid, covered, in the refrigerator.

4 cups water
6-inch piece of dried seaweed (sold in sheets, can be found in Asian and gourmet markets)
4 whole dried black mushrooms (can be found in Asian markets and in the "soup" section of some grocery stores)
2 Tablespoons lemon juice
1 Tablespoon rice syrup
1 teaspoon ground dried ginger
2 teaspoons ground dried garlic
1 pound seitan (gluten), allow to thaw in the refrigerator until soft if purchased frozen

Combine all ingredients (except the seitan) in a 1-gallon pot and bring to a fast boil. Reduce heat and allow mixture to simmer for 30 minutes before adding seitan.

Cut the seitan first into desired shapes (see next page for suggestions). Remember, seitan expands a lot, so whatever shape you cut, make the pieces at least half the size you want them to be ultimately.

Variations:

-For "scallops," shape the raw seitan into a long roll about 1-2 inches in diameter. Cut into coin shapes. Drop into boiling cooking liquid and simmer 30 minutes. Refrigerate overnight in the cooking liquid.

-For "fish," flatten the raw seitan into very thin fillet shapes and cook in the cooking broth at a low boil, rather than a simmer, for 30 minutes to make a softer product. Refrigerate overnight in the cooking liquid.

-For "clams," rip the raw seitan into 1-inch pieces. Bring the cooking liquid to a boil and drop in the gluten pieces. Boil 3 minutes and refrigerate overnight in the cooking liquid.

Note: Once you have cooked "seafood," you can add it to hot soups, stews, pastas, and casseroles. You may let it cool and add it to cold green, pasta, or vegetable salads. Refrigerate any leftover portions of seitan "seafood" and use within 2 days. You can freeze cooked "seafood," remembering that it will be a bit soggy when thawed.

Total calories per serving: 453
Total Fat as % of Daily Value: 3%   Dietary Fiber: 1 g
Protein: 82 g   Fat: 2 g
Carbohydrates: 23 g   Calcium: 170 mg
Iron: 7.1 mg   Sodium: 81 mg

"SEAFOOD" FOR BRUNCH: KEDEGEREE

Serves 4

Kedegeree is an English dish adapted from a traditional Indian breakfast soup. It makes a great brunch, lunch, or supper dish. Instead of the traditional smoked fish, we use smoked tofu.

1½ cups long grain white rice or quick-cooking brown rice
2 cups vegetable broth
¼ cup water
Vegetable oil spray
½ cup diced sweet onion
2 cups chopped smoked tofu
2 teaspoons curry powder
½ teaspoon kelp powder (if available)
½ cup minced fresh parsley
½ cup soymilk
1 teaspoon white pepper
⅛ teaspoon hot sauce

In a medium-size saucepan, bring the rice, broth, and water to a boil. Cover, and allow to simmer for 10-15 minutes or until all the liquid is absorbed.

While the rice is cooking, spray a skillet with oil and sauté the onion for 3 minutes or until soft. Add the smoked tofu, curry powder, and kelp powder (if available). Sauté for 2 minutes. Add the parsley, cooked rice, soymilk, white pepper, and hot sauce. Stir and cook until the soymilk is absorbed. Serve hot.

Total calories per serving: 431
Total Fat as % of Daily Value: 16%   Dietary Fiber: 4 g
Protein: 20 g   Fat: 10 g
Carbohydrates: 68 g   Calcium: 261 mg
Iron: 4.8 mg   Sodium: 447 mg

"TUNA" NOODLE CASSEROLE
Serves 5

¾ cup wheat or rice pasta, such as rotini, spirals, elbows, or bow ties
Vegetable oil spray
1 cup sliced fresh button mushrooms
½ cup minced onions
1 clove garlic, minced
½ cup minced celery
1 cup vegan sour cream combined with ½ cup soymilk
1 cup frozen (thawed) green peas
1 cup chunked vegan "tuna" (thawed if frozen)
2 Tablespoons chopped pimentos
1 teaspoon white pepper
½ teaspoon kelp powder (optional)
1 cup fresh breadcrumbs
2 Tablespoons nutritional yeast
1 teaspoon paprika

Preheat oven to 375 degrees. Cook the pasta until al dente (very chewy) and drain and set aside. Spray skillet with oil. Sauté the mushrooms, onion, garlic, and celery in the oil over medium heat until soft.

Place pasta and vegetables in a large bowl. Mix in vegan sour cream, soymilk, peas, vegan "tuna," pimentos, pepper, and kelp powder until combined. Top with breadcrumbs, nutritional yeast, and paprika. Bake uncovered 30-35 minutes or until bubbly, then serve.

Total calories per serving: 499
Total Fat as % of Daily Value: 38%   Dietary Fiber: 6 g
Protein: 16 g   Fat: 25 g
Carbohydrates: 56 g   Calcium: 94 mg
Iron: 4.2 mg   Sodium: 914 mg

SPICY "FISH" CAKES
Makes 18 cakes or 9 servings

Serve with hot salsa or vegan tartar sauce (vegan mayonnaise combined with diced onions, minced pickles, and lemon juice). Or serve as a "fish" burger on a toasted bun with vegan tartar sauce and sliced tomatoes, cucumber, and Romaine lettuce.

"Seafood" Seasoning (makes approximately ¼ cup dry mix):
   3 Tablespoons broken dried bay leaves
   1 Tablespoon salt
   2 Tablespoons dry mustard
   1 Tablespoon white pepper
   1 Tablespoon ground black pepper
   1 Tablespoon paprika
   1 teaspoon powdered ginger
   1 teaspoon red pepper flakes
   ¼ teaspoon ground cloves
   ¼ teaspoon ground black cardamom (optional)

Place all ingredients for "Seafood" Seasoning in a coffee or spice grinder. Process until all seasonings are well blended and a powder is formed. Store in an airtight container.

Vegan "Fish" Cakes:
   1½ pounds mashed firm tofu
   1 pound baking potatoes that have been peeled, boiled or
      steamed, and mashed
   ½ cup finely minced onion
   ½ cup fresh breadcrumbs (fresh bread torn into small
      pieces or cut into small squares)
   2 Tablespoons "Seafood" Seasoning (see recipe above)
   2 Tablespoons soy sauce (lower sodium soy sauce is fine)
   2 Tablespoons lemon juice
   2 teaspoons minced fresh garlic
   ¼ cup minced fresh parsley

Vegan Seafood

Place all ingredients in a medium-size bowl and mix together until well combined. Form into 18 patties and place on plates. Cover and chill for at least 1 hour.

Vegan "Fish" Cake Breading:
- 1 cup unbleached or whole wheat flour
- ¼ cup crumbled dried seaweed, such as nori (if not available, use dried parsley)
- 1 Tablespoon nutritional yeast
- 1 Tablespoon "Seafood" Seasoning (recipe above)
- 1 teaspoon garlic powder
- 1 teaspoon red pepper flakes

Place all ingredients in the canister of a blender or food processor. Process until well mixed.

To prepare vegan "fish" cakes, preheat oven to 400 degrees. Dredge cakes in breading mixture. Place on nonstick baking pans or spray pans with vegetable oil. Bake 10-12 minutes or until bottoms are brown. Turn over and bake about 5 minutes longer or until browned on both sides.

Note: You may spray baking cakes with vegetable oil for a crisper coating. See variations for this recipe on the next page!

Total calories per serving: 187
Total Fat as % of Daily Value: 6%   Dietary Fiber: 4 g
Protein: 11 g   Fat: 4 g
Carbohydrates: 29 g   Calcium: 195 mg
Iron: 3.3 mg   Sodium: 196 mg

Spicy "Fish" Cake variations: If you would like different flavors, add the following to the "fish" cake (see page 54) mixture before cooking:

Thai "Fish" Cakes: 1 Tablespoon red chile paste, 2 cloves garlic (crushed), ¼ teaspoon ground cinnamon.

"Fish" and Chips Flavor: 1 Tablespoon vinegar, 2 teaspoons sugar, 2 Tablespoons minced pickles (garlic or dill, not sweet).

Southeast Indian "Fish" Cakes: 1 Tablespoon grated fresh ginger, 2 Tablespoons minced fresh cilantro, 1 Tablespoon minced fresh mint, 1 clove garlic (minced), $1/8$ teaspoon curry powder, $1/8$ teaspoon turmeric, $1/8$ teaspoon ground coriander, $1/8$ teaspoon cayenne.

For More Heat "Fish" Cakes: 2 Tablespoons chopped fresh or canned jalapeño, 1 teaspoon ground ginger, 1 teaspoon hot sauce.

"FISH" CAKES
Serves 6

Serve these savory patties as an entrée, accompanied by a crisp green salad and grilled veggies, or as part of a picnic meal with coleslaw or potato salad.

1 cup crumbled extra-firm tofu
1 cup crumbled "fish" fillets (see recipe on page 48)
¼ cup chopped fresh parsley
1 Tablespoon fresh dill
2 Tablespoons lemon juice
1 Tablespoon drained capers
2 Tablespoons dried, chopped canned pimentos

Place all ingredients in the canister of a food processor. Process until well combined. Refrigerate for at least 40 minutes.

Form into cakes; size is your preference. The cakes can be served chilled with your favorite creamy salad dressing, or baked in a 400 degree oven for 10 minutes. They can also be pan-fried until the outside is crispy.

Total calories per serving: 165
Total Fat as % of Daily Value: 9%   Dietary Fiber: 2.5 g
Protein: 15 g   Fat: 6 g
Carbohydrates: 16 g   Calcium: 162 mg
Iron: 3.7 mg   Sodium: 132 mg

BOURRIDE
Serves 6

A vegetable and "fish" stew thickened with potatoes.

2 large baking potatoes (about 2 pounds)
3 cloves garlic, mashed
¼ cup olive oil
Vegetable oil spray
½ cup julienned onions
½ cup julienned carrots
¼ cup julienned leeks
1½ cups frozen, thawed peas
1 cup white wine (or ½ cup white vinegar)
2 cups vegetable stock
2½ pounds (4¼ cups) extra-firm tofu or smoked tofu,
    cut into "steaks"

Preheat oven to 400 degrees. Bake potatoes until very tender. Peel potatoes while hot and place in a food processor or blender. Process until puréed. Add garlic and olive oil and mix to combine. The mixture will resemble a thick mayonnaise. Set aside.

Spray a large frying pan with oil and heat. Sauté onions, carrots, and leeks until tender, about 5 minutes. Set aside. If necessary, cook peas to thaw. Drain and set aside.

Place wine or vinegar and stock in a deep soup pot. Cook over high heat until half the liquid is evaporated. Place tofu in the liquid and heat gently for 5 minutes. Remove tofu and set aside.

Allow the remaining liquid to cook until it is evaporated by half. Stir in the potatoes and allow stew to cook until hot, about 5 minutes.

To serve, place potatoes on bottom of serving dish. Arrange tofu, vegetable mixture, and peas on top of potatoes and serve.

Variation: You can use vegan "shrimp" instead of the tofu.

Total calories per serving: 311
Total Fat as % of Daily Value: 16%   Dietary Fiber: 5 g
Protein: 21 g   Fat: 10 g
Carbohydrates: 37 g   Calcium: 325 mg
Iron: 5.2 mg   Sodium: 352 mg

Vegan Seafood

FRAGRANT "SHRIMP" OR "CRAB" IN COCONUT MILK STEW

Serves 6

Vegetable oil spray
2 Tablespoons minced shallots
4 Tablespoons chopped fresh cilantro
1 ½ Tablespoons minced fresh ginger
1 teaspoon poppy seeds
½ teaspoon ground cloves
¼ teaspoon ground cinnamon
¼ teaspoon turmeric
One 4-inch piece of lemongrass
1 ¼ pounds vegan "shrimp" or "crab" (about 2 ½ cups)
14-ounce can lowfat coconut milk (about 1 ½ cups)
1 cup vegan sour cream
2 ½ cups peeled, diced potatoes, cooked
1 cup frozen, thawed peas

Spray a large pot with oil. Sweat shallots only until they glisten, about 1-2 minutes. Add cilantro, ginger, poppy seeds, cloves, cinnamon, turmeric, and lemongrass. Sauté for 3 minutes.

Add vegan "shrimp" or "crab" while stirring and sauté for 3 minutes or until vegan "shrimp" or "crab" is heated. Stir in coconut milk and allow mixture to simmer for 5 minutes.

Whisk in sour cream and bring to a fast boil. Reduce heat and simmer for 10 minutes or until flavors are married. Keep warm.

Allow potatoes and peas to come to room temperature. If necessary, microwave or steam only long enough to warm them.

To serve stew, divide potatoes and peas into individual dishes. Pour "shrimp" or "crab" mixture over potatoes and peas and serve hot.

Total calories per serving: 398
Total Fat as % of Daily Value: 36%
Protein: 6 g
Carbohydrates: 44 g
Iron: 2.7 mg

Dietary Fiber: 4 g
Fat: 25 g
Calcium: 34 mg
Sodium: 2,586 mg ("crab" is high in sodium)

VEGAN "CRAB" RAGOON

Serves 12 (appetizers) or 6 (entrées)

This entrée is a "blast from the past," considered very elegant in the 1930's through the 1950's. It is currently making a comeback.

> **Vegetable oil spray**
> **24 vegan wonton wrappers (rice paper will work, too)**
> **1 Tablespoon Chinese Five-Spice Seasoning (optional)**
> **1 ¼ cups shredded vegan "crab"**
> **1 cup vegan cream cheese**
> **1 Tablespoon chopped onion**
> **¼ cup chopped green onion**
> **2 teaspoons soy sauce**
> **2 teaspoons minced fresh ginger**
> **1 teaspoon white pepper**

Preheat the oven to 350 degrees. Spray 2 baking sheets with oil. On a plate, separate wonton wrappers or rice papers and sprinkle with Five-Spice Seasoning, if using. Set aside.

In a large bowl, combine remaining ingredients and mix thoroughly. Set aside.

Cut one wonton or rice paper diagonally so that it forms 2 triangles. Continue with the remaining wrappers or rice papers. Arrange the wrappers/papers on the baking sheets in a single layer. Place in the oven and bake until just brown about 5 minutes. Remove and cool.

Place the cream cheese mixture in a small baking dish or 1-quart oven-proof bowl. Bake until the cream cheese is heated and just starting to bubble, about 15 minutes. Remove and portion onto dinner plates, topping with wontons.

Serve accompanied by a fresh fruit or green salad. You can also place the baked wontons on plates, and portion the "crab"-cream cheese mixture over them.

Total calories per entrée serving: 379

Total Fat as % of Daily Value: 23%	Dietary Fiber: 2 g
Protein: 8 g	Fat: 16 g
Carbohydrates: 53 g	Calcium: 41 mg
Iron: 2.6 mg	Sodium: 1,841 mg ("crab" is high in sodium)

Vegan Seafood

"FISH" TACOS
Serves 6

¼ cup fresh lime juice
1 Tablespoon vegetable oil
1 Tablespoon cumin powder
1 Tablespoon chili powder
½ Tablespoon ground dried oregano
1 teaspoon white pepper
5 vegan "fish" fillets (see recipe on page 48)
6 flour or whole wheat tortillas (8-inch diameter)
2 cups drained, canned black beans (or cooked, fresh)
1 cup prepared salsa
1 cup shredded vegan soy cheese (Monterey Jack or
   Cheddar)
1 cup vegan soy sour cream

In a large bowl combine lime juice, oil, cumin, chili powder, oregano, and pepper; stir well. Add "fish" to marinade, cover, and refrigerate for at least 30 minutes.

Preheat oven to 400 degrees. Place "fish" with marinade in a baking dish. Wrap tortillas in foil. Place "fish" and tortillas in oven and allow to heat for 10 minutes.

While fish is heating, put black beans in a microwave-safe dish, cover and heat on HIGH in the microwave for 3 minutes. Remove "fish" and tortillas from oven. Assemble by placing a piece of "fish" in the center of each warm tortilla. Top with beans. salsa, shredded cheese, and sour cream.

Total calories per serving: 583
Total Fat as % of Daily Value: 37%
Protein: 26 g
Carbohydrates: 69 g
Iron: 8.5 mg

Dietary Fiber: 9 g
Fat: 14 g
Calcium: 144 mg
Sodium: 781 mg

ETHIOPIAN-STYLE "SHRIMP" AND SWEET POTATO STEW

Serves 6

I cup water
I cup chopped sweet onions
3 Tablespoons fresh chopped and seeded chilies (you
  choose the heat)
2 teaspoons minced fresh ginger
2 cloves garlic, minced
2 teaspoons ground cumin
¼ teaspoon ground cinnamon
2 teaspoons red pepper flakes
3 fresh peeled and small-diced sweet potatoes (about
  3 cups)
3 cups diced canned tomatoes
2 cups drained canned garbanzo beans
I cup fresh, or frozen, thawed green beans (cut in I-inch
  pieces)
I½ cups vegetable broth
¼ cup peanut butter
2 cups vegan "shrimp"
½ cup chopped fresh cilantro or parsley

Put water, onion, chilies, ginger, and garlic in a large pot. Cook over high heat, stirring occasionally, for 5 minutes. Add cumin, cinnamon, and red pepper. Cook and stir for 1 minute. Add sweet potatoes, tomatoes, garbanzo beans, green beans, vegetable broth, and peanut butter. Bring to a boil, reduce heat and simmer for 30 minutes or until potatoes are tender. Stir in "shrimp" and cilantro and cook for 5 minutes. Serve over steamed rice.

Note: If peanut butter is not desired, you may substitute ¼ cup vegan cream cheese or ¼ cup coconut milk.

Total calories per serving: 316
Total Fat as % of Daily Value: 13%
Protein: 10 g
Carbohydrates: 50 g
Iron: 4 mg

Dietary Fiber: 9 g
Fat: 9 g
Calcium: 121 mg
Sodium: 1,048 mg

VEGAN "CRAB" ENCHILADAS

Serves 6 (2 each)

Vegetable oil spray
1 pound vegan shredded "crab" (about 2¼ cups)
1 cup thinly sliced onion
¾ cup thinly sliced green bell peppers
¼ cup sliced black olives
1½ cups cooked refried beans (or cooked, mashed
red beans)
12 small corn tortillas
1 cup canned tomatoes diced in juice (not drained)
½ cup shredded vegan cheddar cheese (if desired)

Preheat oven to 350 degrees. Spray a large skillet with oil and allow to heat. Sauté crab, onion, pepper, and olives in skillet. Stir in beans. Stir well and simmer over low heat.

Spoon mixture into tortillas, roll up tortillas, and place into shallow baking pan. Top evenly with tomatoes. Bake for 20 minutes or until thoroughly heated.

If desired, top with vegan shredded cheese and allow to bake for an additional 5 minutes or until cheese is bubbly.

Total calories per serving: 322
Total Fat as % of Daily Value: 9%   Dietary Fiber: 10 g
Protein: 12 g   Fat: 7 g
Carbohydrates: 59 g   Calcium: 133 mg
Iron: 3.8 mg   Sodium: 2,210 mg ("crab" is high in sodium)

Answers to FAQ (or comments) About Eating Fish

By Reed Mangels, PhD, RD

"I think of fish as a good lowfat source of protein."

Fact: There are many vegetarian protein sources that are at least as lowfat as most fish and are higher in fiber. For example, a cup of lentils has as much protein as 3 ounces of broiled Atlantic salmon and has less than 10% as much fat and saturated fat. The table on the next page shows the serving size of vegetarian foods that you would need to get as much protein as would be in a 3-ounce serving of fresh salmon or water-packed tuna. As you can see, the vegetarian options are typically lower in fat and saturated fat and higher in fiber. In some cases the vegetarian foods are higher in calories but they also supply more fiber and phytochemicals than fish do.

Product	Svg. Size	Protein (grams)	Fat (grams)	Saturated Fat (grams)	Fiber (grams)	Calories
Atlantic Salmon, broiled	3 ounces	19	10.5	2.1	0	175
Water-packed Tuna	3 ounces	19	2.4	0.6	0	118
Veggie burger	1-1/2 burgers	19	0.8	0	6	105
Lentils	1 cup + 1 TB	19	0.8	0.1	16.5	243
Black Beans	1-1/4 cups	19	1.2	0.3	18.7	284
Kidney Beans	1-1/4 cups	19	1.1	0.2	14.2	281
Tofu Dog	2	18	0	0	2	90
Tofurky Jurky	6 slices	18	0	0	1.5	150
Veggie Deli Slices	4-3/4 slices	19	2.6	0	0	118

"Usually I don't eat fish but now that I'm pregnant, I'm worried that my baby will be missing something if I don't eat fish."

Fact: Actually, you may be doing your baby a favor by not eating fish. Fish can contain high levels of environmental toxins like mercury, PCBs, and dioxin. Fish that live in the ocean and are long-lived predators like tuna, swordfish, and sharks, may have especially high levels of mercury that will be passed on to anyone eating those fish.

Mercury is especially harmful to fetuses and young children. The U.S. Food and Drug Administration recommends that pregnant women and women who could become pregnant avoid eating shark, king mackerel, tilefish, and swordfish and recommends limiting the amount of other fish eaten (FDA). PCBs and dioxin are concentrated in fatty fish and then are passed on to people when they eat fish. PCBs affect the developing nervous system. Several studies have shown that vegetarians have markedly lower levels of PCBs, DDT, and other contaminants in their breast milk than do women who eat meat or women who eat fatty fish (Sanders, Hergenrather, Noren). Since fish is not an essential part of the diet, why take a chance? Vegetarian foods can provide protein and other nutrients found in fish. DHA, or docosahexaenoic acid, found in fish oil is now available as a vegan supplement derived from microalgae. If you want to learn more about DHA, see page 71.

"Lately I have been craving fish (especially tuna and salmon). Could I be missing something in my diet or could it be due to allergies?"

Fact: There is no evidence that people crave foods because of vitamin or mineral deficiencies or because of allergies. No one knows for sure why people "crave" certain foods but it may be because they see the food often and miss eating it or because they are bored with the foods they usually eat and are looking for something different. Perhaps it is the salty taste of tuna and salmon that you are missing. You could try eating some saltier protein containing foods like veggie burgers and deli slices (unless you are on a low sodium diet for medical reasons) to see if that helps.

It is important to make sure that your diet is nutritionally adequate and that you are getting enough calories. Sometimes what feels like a craving is simply hunger due to an inadequate diet. An appointment with a registered dietitian who is supportive of vegetarianism could help you make sure that your diet is nutritionally adequate.

"It's just so simple to grill fish or open a can of tuna."

Fact: Vegetarian meals can be as simple to prepare as you choose. For instance, instead of opening a can of tuna, why not open a can of chickpeas or try the mock tuna salad recipe on page 38? If you're looking for simple dinners, check out The Vegetarian Resource Group's *Simply Vegan* and *Conveniently Vegan* for lots of quick, easy ideas. Also go to http://www.vrg.org/journal/vj2003issue1/vj2003issue1quick.htm

"I only eat fish when I go out to a restaurant."

Fact: These days, most restaurants offer vegetarian choices. If you're feeling like fish is your only option, you may need to look at other restaurants. Try Chinese, Ethiopian, Thai, and Indian restaurants if you're looking for a wider variety of vegetarian selections. If you're not sure what a restaurant can offer, call ahead and speak to the chef or manager. They will often be happy to create a vegetarian entrée just for you that would be the envy of your dining companions.

References

USDHHS and USEPA. What you need to know about mercury in fish and shellfish. March 2004. http://www.cfsan.fda.gov/~dms/admehg3.html.

Sanders TAB, Reddy S. The influence of a vegetarian diet on the fatty acid composition of human milk and the essential fatty acid status of the infant. *J Pediatr.* 1992;120:S71-7.

Hergenrather J, Hlady G, Wallace B, Savage E. Pollutants in breast milk of vegetarians. *N Engl J Med.* 1981;304:792.

Noren K. Levels of organochlorine contaminants in human milk in relation to the dietary habits of the mothers. *Acta Paediatr Scand.* 1983;72:811-816.

Fish and the Environment

If you're interested in learning more about the environmental impact of eating fish, one place to start is with Erik Marcus' book *Meat Market* (pages 201-207). Marcus' section on fishing concludes, "Avoiding seafood is an acknowledgement that the oceans are under tremendous pressure, and that we each have the ability to avoid contributing to the problem." Marcus E. *Meat Market.* Animals, Ethics, and Money. Ithaca, NY: Brio Press; 2005. You may also be interested in Jeanne Bartas' article on aquaculture. See http://www.vrg.org/journal/vj97may/975aqua.htm

Question About Fish Oil

By Reed Mangels, PhD, RD

I am a vegan and am concerned about heart disease. I have read that fish oil is an important part of a diet to prevent heart disease. Do I need to use fish oil?

A number of studies have looked at the benefits of eating fish or using fish oil to reduce the risk of heart disease. Recently, researchers combined the results of studies involving more than 200,000 individuals and found that, compared with those who never ate fish or those who ate fish less than once a month, those eating fish once per week had a 15 percent reduced risk of dying from heart disease, while those eating fish 5 or more times per week had almost a 40 percent reduction in risk.[1] Each 20 gram-per-day increase in fish intake was related to a 7 percent lower risk of dying from heart disease.[1]

Results like these have led some medical experts to recommend that people eat fatty fish or use fish oil supplements. In early September 2004, The Food and Drug Administration approved a qualified health claim for foods containing omega-3 fatty acids, mainly fatty fish. The labels on these foods can now say,

> *"Supportive but not conclusive research shows that consumption of EPA and DHA omega-3 fatty acids may reduce the risk of coronary heart disease...."*

The FDA approved a similar statement for dietary supplements containing EPA and DHA omega-3 fatty acids, earlier.

These results showing a benefit of fish oil or fatty fish may not apply to vegetarians, however. Vegetarian diets contain a number of protective factors, and fish oil may not convey any added benefits. Most studies showing positive effects of fish consumption have compared diets high in fish to diets high in meat.

It makes sense that replacing saturated fat- and cholesterol-laden meat with fish would provide health benefits for the general public. Would vegetarians who are already eating healthful diets experience similar benefits if they added fish or fish oil? We don't really know, but several studies show that vegetarian diets compare favorably with diets that include fish:

- In a large study from the United Kingdom, lacto-ovo vegetarians and fish-eaters had similar blood cholesterol levels. Vegans had the lowest levels of cholesterol, and meat-eaters had the highest levels.[2]

- Similarly, high blood pressure was most common in meat-eaters. Lacto-ovo vegetarians and fish-eaters had intermediate levels of high blood pressure, and vegans had the lowest prevalence of high blood pressure.[3]

- Mortality from heart disease was 20 percent lower in occasional meat-eaters, 34 percent lower in those who ate fish but not meat, 34 percent lower in lacto-ovo vegetarians, and 26 percent lower in vegans compared to regular meat-eaters.[4] The number of vegans was small, though; these results should not be used to suggest that a vegan diet isn't as good as a diet that includes fish or dairy products.

Fatty fish and fish oil contain 2 unusual kinds of fats, docosahexaenoic acid (DHA for short) and eicosapentaenoic acid (EPA). These fats, along with alpha-linolenic acid, are in a group of fats called omega-3 fats. EPA and DHA are often cited as being the beneficial components of fish oil.

EPA and DHA are not considered to be essential for humans because we are able to produce them from alpha-linolenic acid, which is an essential fat. The question of how much EPA and DHA we are able to make from alpha-linolenic acid is an area that is being researched and debated. It does appear, however, that some conversion does occur, so it is important for vegans and vegetarians to include sources of alpha-linolenic acid in their diet on a regular basis. These sources include flax seed, flax seed oil, canola oil, soy products, hemp products, and walnuts.

Avoiding trans fats (from food like margarine and commercial baked goods containing hydrogenated fats) can help to keep these fats from interfering with EPA and DHA production. Using less sunflower, safflower, corn, and sesame oils and more soybean, canola, and olive oils can also help to encourage DHA and EPA production. Since we are not certain what other factors influence how much EPA and DHA an individual can produce from alpha-linolenic acid, some people opt to use DHA supplements from microalgae as a simple way of insuring adequate intake. While the type of dietary fat is one factor that can reduce risk of heart disease, there are other important steps vegans and vegetarians can take to promote heart health. These include:

- Exercising regularly

- Avoiding obesity

- Eating a variety of plant foods to supply fiber, antioxidants, and phytochemicals

- Being sure to get adequate vitamin B_{12}, folate, and vitamin B_6 to help keep blood homocysteine levels low

- Eating less saturated fat, trans fats, and cholesterol

References

1   He K, Song Y, Daviglus ML, et al. 2004. Accumulated evidence on fish consumption and coronary heart disease mortality: a meta-analysis of cohort studies. *Circulation* 109:2705-11.

2   Appleby PN, Thorogood M, Mann JI, Key TJA. 1999. The Oxford Vegetarian Study: an overview. *Am J Clin Nutr* 70 (suppl):525S-31S.

3   Appleby PN, Davey GK, Key TJ. 2002. Hypertension and blood pressure among meat eaters, fish eaters, vegetarians and vegans in EPIC-Oxford. *Public Health Nutr* 5:645-54.

4   Key TJ, Fraser GE, Thorogood M, et al. 1999. Mortality in vegetarians and nonvegetarians: detailed findings from a collaborative analysis of 5 prospective studies. *Am J Clin Nutr* 70 (suppl):516S-24S.

Questions and Answers about Omega-3 Fatty Acids for Vegans

By Reed Mangels, PhD, RD

Omega-3 fatty acids are showing up in all sorts of products. I took a quick trip down the aisles of a grocery store and a natural foods store and found cereals, soymilk, pasta, snack bars, and even peanut butter proudly proclaiming "contains omega-3 fatty acids." Labels and ads trumpet, "Omega-3 DHA is an important brain nutrient," and "Omega-3s may reduce the risk of heart disease." Are these claims real or are they hype? Should vegans be concerned about omega-3 fatty acids? We'll look at these questions and more.

What are omega-3 fatty acids?

Omega-3 fatty acids are polyunsaturated fatty acids—building blocks of fats. They differ from other fatty acids because of the number of carbons that they contain and where double bonds are located. The omega-3 fatty acids that are most important nutritionally are alpha-linolenic acid, docosahexaenoic acid, and eicosapentaenoic acid (DHA and EPA for short).

Why are omega-3 fatty acids important?

Our bodies cannot make alpha-linolenic acid, so it is essential for us to get it from our diet. We can make DHA and EPA from alpha-linolenic acid, although there are some questions about how efficient this process is. Some have suggested that DHA should be considered an essential fatty acid.[1] Recent research on omega-3 fatty acids has focused on the following areas:

Pregnancy and Breastfeeding

A higher intake of omega-3 fatty acids in pregnancy may slightly reduce the risk of having a premature baby.[2] In addition, DHA is essential for normal brain development[3] and appears to play a role in the development of the infant's vision. The amount of DHA in a woman's diet determines the amount of DHA that appears in her breastmilk.

Heart Disease

A number of studies have found that risk of death from heart disease is lower in people with higher intakes of omega-3 fatty acids. Omega-3 fatty acids may also reduce risk of stroke and reduce elevated blood pressure.[4] (For more information on omega-3 fatty acids and heart disease, see the *Nutrition Hotline* column in Issue 1, 2005, of *Vegetarian Journal*, which is available at <www.vrg.org/journal/vj2005issue1/vj2005issue1hotline.htm>.

Depression

People with clinical depression tend to have lower blood concentrations of omega-3 fatty acids than non-depressed controls. In some studies, one gram of EPA (either with or without DHA) has been used, along with antidepressants, to treat people with depression.[5]

Other Conditions

EPA and DHA appear to have some benefits for those with rheumatoid arthritis, including reduction of morning stiffness and pain relief. They may be beneficial in other conditions like Crohn's disease, Alzheimer's disease, and asthma, but there is not yet enough research in these areas to make recommendations.[6,7]

Which foods contain DHA and EPA?

Vegetarian diets contain low levels of EPA and DHA, mainly from dairy products and eggs; vegan diets do not normally contain EPA or DHA. The only plant sources of EPA and DHA are microalgae and sea vegetables. Sea vegetables are not a concentrated source of these omega-3 fatty acids and do not provide significant amounts of omega-3 fatty acids for most people. Fish, especially fatty fish, do have DHA and EPA. This is not because the fish produce these fatty acids but because the fish eat microalgae containing DHA and EPA. A vegan DHA made from microalgae has been developed and is being added to some foods and used to make supplements.

Must we get DHA and EPA from food, or can our bodies produce these omega-3 fatty acids? Do vegans get enough DHA and EPA?

Our bodies are able to produce some DHA and EPA from alpha-linolenic acid, but we are not very efficient at this production. The rate of conversion is low in women and very low in men.[3] Vegans who do not use DHA supplements or eat DHA-fortified foods must rely on conversion of alpha-linolenic acid to DHA and EPA. Some studies have found that blood levels of EPA and DHA are lower in vegans and vegetarians than in meat-eaters.[8,9] Whether or not these lower levels have health consequences is not known. The concentration of DHA in breastmilk from vegan women is lower than that in lacto-ovo vegetarians or non-vegetarians.[10,11] Milk EPA concentration can be increased if dietary alpha-linolenic acid intake increases, but milk DHA content remains unchanged.[12]

How can vegans maximize DHA and EPA production?

- Include sources of alpha-linolenic acid in your diet on a regular basis. Major sources include ground flaxseed, flaxseed oil, canola oil, soy products, hemp products, and walnuts. Green leafy vegetables, sea vegetables, and pecans also provide smaller amounts of alpha-linolenic acid. (See chart on next page.)

- Whole flaxseeds are not easily digested, so the alpha-linolenic acid that they contain is not available to us. If you are using flaxseeds as a source of alpha-linolenic acid, be sure to use ground or milled flaxseeds or flaxseed oil.

- Avoid trans fats since they interfere with EPA and DHA production. Trans fats are found in foods containing hydrogenated fat, like margarine and commercial cookies and crackers.

- Use less sunflower, safflower, corn, and sesame oil and more soybean, canola, and olive oil to promote DHA and EPA production. Sunflower, safflower, corn, and sesame oil are high in linoleic acid, an omega-6 fatty acid that can interfere with DHA and EPA production.

Alpha-Linolenic Acid in Foods

FOOD, SERVING SIZE	ALPHA-LINOLENIC ACID (Milligrams/Serving)
Avocado, ½	125
Breakfast cereal with flax and/or hemp, 1 serving*	400-1,000
Broccoli, cooked, 1 cup	190
Cabbage, cooked, 1 cup	165
Canola oil, 1 teaspoon	400
Collards, cooked, 1 cup	180
Flaxseed oil, 1 teaspoon	2,400
Flaxseed, ground, 1 teaspoon*	570
Hot cereal containing flax, 1 serving*	450
Kale, cooked, 1 cup	130
Pasta containing flax, 1 serving*	600
Peanut butter containing flaxseed oil, 2 Tablespoons	1,000
Pecans, ¼ cup	240
Snack bar containing flax and/or hemp, 1 bar*	400-2,100
Soybean oil, 1 teaspoon	300
Soybeans, cooked, ½ cup	320-510
Soymilk, 1 cup	210
Soy nuts, ¼ cup	725
Tempeh, 3 ounces	120
Tofu, ½ cup	400
Walnuts, ¼ cup	2,270-2,700
Walnut oil, 1 teaspoon	470

*Flaxseed should be ground or milled; otherwise little or no alpha-linolenic acid will be absorbed.

Sources: Composition of Foods. USDA Nutrient Data Base for Standard Reference, Release 18, 2005, and manufacturers' information.

What about supplements of omega-3 fatty acids?

Alpha-linolenic acid supplements produce a small increase in blood EPA concentrations but do not increase concentrations of DHA in the blood.[13] These results have led some researchers to recommend direct supplementation with DHA for some groups with increased needs for EPA and DHA (pregnant and breastfeeding women) or with a risk for low conversion of alpha-linolenic acid to EPA and DHA (people with diabetes, premature infants).[8,14] DHA supplements can increase blood concentrations of both DHA and EPA.

Supplements with both EPA and DHA also are effective in increasing blood levels of EPA and DHA.[15]

What amount of omega-3 fatty acids do we need?

There is limited storage of omega-3 fatty acids in our bodies, so these fatty acids should be a regular part of the diet.[15] When you are thinking about the amount of omega-3 fatty acids that you should be getting, one key question is whether you are relying on alpha-linolenic acid being converted to EPA and DHA or taking a direct source of DHA.

If you are a vegan relying only on alpha-linolenic acid as the source of omega-3 fatty acids, approximately 1-2 percent of calories should come from alpha-linolenic acid.[15] For the typical adult man, this would be 2,200-5,300 milligrams (2.2-5.3 grams) of alpha-linolenic acid; for the typical adult woman, 1,800-4,400 milligrams (1.8-4.4 grams). Very active and heavier people as well as pregnant and lactating women should strive for the higher end of the range; smaller and more sedentary people should aim towards the lower end.

If you are using a supplement or foods that contain DHA or EPA on a daily basis, strive for the adequate intake for alpha-linolenic acid established by the Institute of Medicine of 1.6 grams per day for men and 1.1 grams per day for women.[3]

There is no Recommended Daily Allowance (RDA) for EPA or DHA, but the American Heart Association recommends 500-1,800 milligrams (0.5-1.8 grams) per day of DHA and/or EPA to significantly reduce the risk of death from heart disease.[17] This level seems appropriate for people with a family history of heart disease, although there have been no studies examining whether DHA supplements further reduce the risk of death from heart disease in vegans.

Because of DHA's role in infant development, several groups[2,18] have suggested that pregnant and lactating women get 200-300 milligrams (0.2-0.3 grams) of DHA daily from fortified food or supplements.

Vegan DHA and DHA + EPA Supplements

- O-Mega-Zen 3 300 mg DHA/capsule —www.nutru.com
- Dr. Fuhrman's DHA Purity 175 mg DHA/0.5 ml — www.drfuhrman.com/shop/DHA.aspx
- Vegan Omega-3 DHA 200 mg DHA/capsule — www.devanutrition.com
- V-Pure Omega-3 135 mg DHA + 37.5 mg EPA/capsule — www.water4.net/products.htm

Vegan Foods Containing DHA
Derived from Microalgae

- California Veggie Burger 42 mg DHA/1 burger; www.veggiepatch.com
- Odwalla Soymilk 32 mg DHA/8-ounce serving; www.odwalla.com
- Odwalla Soy Smart Soymilk Drink 32 mg DHA/8-ounce serving; www.odwalla.com
- Silk Plus Omega-3 Soymilk 32 mg DHA/8-ounce serving; http://omega3.silksoymilkplus.com/

Can someone get too much of the Omega-3 fatty acids?

There is not enough information available to set a safe upper limit for omega-3 fatty acids. The Food and Drug Administration (FDA) says up to 3 grams (3,000 milligrams) per day of EPA + DHA is generally recognized as safe.[19] DHA and EPA may have negative effects on the immune system and may inhibit blood clotting, so supplementation should only be pursued with caution. More is not necessarily better.

Men at risk for prostate cancer should not use high amounts of alpha-linolenic acid since one study found that those men whose diets were highest in alpha-linolenic acid had an increased risk of developing advanced prostate cancer.[20] The other omega-3 fatty acids, EPA and DHA, were associated with lower prostate cancer risk.

Sample Menu That Provides At Least 4,400 Milligrams of Alpha-Linolenic Acid Daily — DAY 1

BREAKFAST:

- 1 bagel with jelly
- 1 medium orange
- 1 cup cold cereal
- 1 cup enriched soymilk

LUNCH:

- Hummus sandwich made with:
  - Hummus (³/₄ cup chickpeas and 2 teaspoons tahini)
  - 3 slices of tomato
  - 2 slices of whole wheat bread
  - 1 medium apple

DINNER:

- 1 cup of cooked pasta with:
  - ¹/₄ cup marinara sauce
  - ¹/₃ cup carrot sticks
  - 1 cup cooked broccoli sautéed in 1 teaspoon canola oil
- 1 whole wheat roll
- A juice pop made with 1 cup frozen grape juice

SNACK:

- ¹/₂ cup trail mix (mix of dates, raisins, and at least 3 Tablespoons of walnuts)
- 1 cup enriched soymilk

Vegan Seafood

Sample Menu That Provides At Least 4,400 Milligrams of Alpha-Linolenic Acid Daily — DAY 2

BREAKFAST:

- 1 serving hot cereal containing milled flaxseed with:
  - 3 Tablespoons wheat germ
  - 1/4 cup raisins or dates
  - 1 ounce chopped walnuts
- 1 cup diced cantaloupe
- 1 cup enriched soymilk

LUNCH:

- Burrito made with:
  - 1 whole wheat tortilla
  - 1/2 cup black beans
  - 1 Tablespoon salsa
- 1 ounce lowfat tortilla chips with:
  - 1/4 cup salsa

DINNER:

- Stir-fry made with:
  - 1/2 cup diced tofu
  - 1 cup vegetables
  - 2 Tablespoons soy sauce
  - 1 1/2 cups cooked quick brown rice
  - 1 teaspoon canola oil
- 3 graham crackers
- 6 ounces calcium-fortified vegetable juice

(Continues on next page!)

SNACK:

- 3 cups popped popcorn with:
  - 1 Tablespoon Vegetarian Support Formula nutritional yeast
- 1 cup enriched soymilk

What's the Bottom Line?

The topic of omega-3 fatty acids, like many topics in nutrition, is fluid. Recommendations change as new studies provide more information. Based on what we know today, here's what you need to remember:

- Alpha-linolenic acid is an essential fatty acid; that means we need to obtain it from food or supplements. To prevent deficiency, vegan adults should have 1-2 percent of calories from alpha-linolenic acid— 2,220-5,300 milligrams of alpha-linolenic acid for the typical adult man, 1,800-4,400 milligrams for the typical adult woman.

- Good sources of alpha-linolenic acid include ground flaxseed, flaxseed oil, canola oil, soy products, hemp products, and walnuts. The table on page 75 provides information about the amount of alpha-linolenic acid in various foods.

- Vegan pregnant and breastfeeding women, people at risk for heart disease or high blood pressure, and people with diabetes are the groups most likely to benefit from supplements of DHA. Approximately 500-1,800 milligrams of DHA has been recommended to reduce the risk of heart disease[17]; 200-300 milligrams of DHA is suggested for pregnant and breastfeeding women.[2,18]

References

1   Gebauer SK, Psota TL, Harris WS, Kris-Etherton PM. 2006. N-3 fatty acid dietary recommendations and food sources to achieve essentiality and cardiovascular benefits. *Am J Clin Nutr* 83(suppl):1526S-35S.

2   Jensen CL. 2006. Effects of n-3 fatty acids during pregnancy and lactation. *Am J Clin Nutr* 83(suppl):1452S-57S.

3   Williams CM, Burdge G. 2006. Long-chain n-3 PUFA: plant v. marine sources. *Proc Nutr Soc* 65:42-50.

4   Food and Nutrition Board, Institute of Medicine. *Dietary Reference Intakes for Energy, Carbohydrate, Fiber, Fat, Fatty Acids, Cholesterol, Protein, and Amino Acids.* Washington: National Academies Press, 2002.

5   Sontrop J, Campbell MK. 2006. Omega-3 polyunsaturated fatty acids and depression: A review of the evidence and a methodological critique. *Prev Med* 42:4-13.

6   Johnson EJ, Schaefer EJ. 2006. Potential role of dietary n-3 fatty acids in the prevention of dementia and macular degeneration. *Am J Clin Nutr* 83(suppl):1494S-98S.

7   Calder PC. 2006. N-3 polyunsaturated fatty acids, inflammation, and inflammatory diseases. *Am J Clin Nutr* 83(suppl):1505S-19S.

8   Davis BC, Kris-Etherton PM. 2003. Achieving optimal essential fatty acid status in vegetarians: current knowledge and practical implications. *Am J Clin Nutr* 78(suppl):640S-46S.

9   Rosell MS, Lloyd-Wright Z, Appleby PN, et al. 2005. Long-chain n-3 polyunsaturated fatty acids in plasma in British meat-eating, vegetarian, and vegan men. *Am J Clin Nutr* 82:327-34.

10 Sanders TAB, Reddy S. 1992. The influence of a vegetarian diet on the fatty acid composition of human milk and the essential fatty acid status of the infant. *J Pediatr* 120:S71-77.

11 Uauy R, Peirano P, Hoffman D, et al. 1996. Role of essential fatty acids in the function of the developing nervous system. *Lipids* 3:S167-S76.

12 Francois CA, Connor SL, Bolewicz LC, Connor WE. 2003. Supplementing lactating women with flaxseed oil does not increase docosahexaenoic acid in their milk. *Am J Clin Nutr* 77:226-33.

13 Harper CR, Edwards MJ, DeFilipis AP, Jacobson TA. 2006. Flaxseed oil increases the plasma concentrations of cardioprotective (n-3) fatty acids in humans. *J Nutr* 136:83-87.

14 Geppert J, Kraft V, Demmelmair H, Koletzko B. 2005. Docosa-hexaenoic acid supplementation in vegetarians effectively increases omega-3 index: a randomized trial. *Lipids* 40:807-14.

15 Arterburn LM, Hall EB, Oken H. 2006. Distribution, interconversion, and dose response of n-3 fatty acids in humans. *Am J Clin Nutr* 83(suppl):1467S-76S.

16 WHO/FAO (World Health Organization/Food and Agriculture Organization). *Diet, Nutrition and the Prevention of Chronic Diseases.* WHO Technical Report Series 916. (Geneva: World Health Organization, 2003.)

17 Kris-Etherton PM, Harris WS, Appel LJ. 2002. AHA Scientific Statement. Fish consumption, fish oil, omega-3 fatty acids, and cardio-vascular disease. *Circulation* 106:2747-57.

18 Melina V, Davis B. *The New Becoming Vegetarian.* Summertown: Book Publishing Company, 2003.

19 Department of Health and Human Services, U.S. Food and Drug Administration. Substances affirmed as generally recognized as safe: menhaden oil. Federal Register. June 5, 1997. Vol. 62, No. 108: pp 30751-30757. 21 CFR Part 184 [Docket No. 86G-0289]. Available at <frwebgate.access.gpo.gov/cgi-bin/getdoc.cgi?dbname=1997 _register&docid=fr05jn97-5>.

20 Leitzmann MF, Stampfer MJ, Michaud DS, et al. 2004. Dietary intake of n-3 and n-6 fatty acids and the risk of prostate cancer. *Am J Clin Nutr* 80:204-16.

**Reed Mangels, PhD, RD, is a Nutrition Advisor
for The Vegetarian Resource Group.
She is the co-author of <u>Simply Vegan</u> and has written
many articles for dietetic and health journals.**

Guide to Resources
from The Vegetarian Resource Group

The following resources can be purchased from The Vegetarian Resource Group, PO Box 1463, Baltimore, MD 21203. You can order online at <www.vrg.org>, or charge your order over the phone by calling (410) 366-8343 between 9 am and 5 pm EST Monday through Friday. An Order Form can be found on page 92.

Shipping and Handling Charges:

Orders under $25	$6 ($10 for Canada/Mexico)
Orders over $25	Free in continental U.S.
Foreign orders	Inquire first

Simply Vegan
Quick Vegetarian Meals

The immensely popular *Simply Vegan*, by Debra Wasserman and Reed Mangels, PhD, RD, is much more than a cookbook. It is a guide to a non-violent, environmentally sound, humane lifestyle. It features over 160 vegan recipes that can be prepared quickly, as well as an extensive nutrition section. The chapters cover topics on protein, fat, calcium, iron, vitamin B_{12}, pregnancy and the vegan diet, and raising vegan kids. Additionally, the book includes sample menus and meal plans. There is also information on cruelty-free shopping, including where to buy vegan food, clothing, cosmetics, household products, and books.

Available for $14.95. (224 pages)

Meatless Meals for Working People

Meatless Meals For Working People, by Debra Wasserman and Charles Stahler contains over 100 delicious fast and easy recipes, plus ideas which teach you to be a vegetarian within your hectic schedule using common convenient vegetarian foods. This handy guide also contains a spice chart, party ideas, information on quick service restaurant chains, and much more.

Available for $12. (192 pages)

Vegan Meals for One or Two

Each recipe in *Vegan Meals for One or Two*, by Nancy Berkoff, EdD, RD, is designed so that you can realistically use ingredients the way they come packaged from the store when cooking for one or two. Meal planning and shopping information is included, as well as breakfast ideas, one-pot wonders, recipes that can be frozen for later use, grab-and-go suggestions, everyday and special occasion entrées, plus desserts and snacks. Sample recipes include Breakfast Potato Burritos, Lentil-Spinach Pilaf, Almost Thai Spicy Peanut Pasta, Asian Sautéed Eggplant, Quick Tofu Stroganoff, Grilled Sweet Onions, and Baked Pears in Apple Cider Syrup. A glossary is provided.

Available for $15. (216 pages)

Conveniently Vegan
Turn Packaged Foods into Delicious Vegetarian Dishes

In *Conveniently Vegan*, by Debra Wasserman, you will learn how to prepare meals with all the new natural foods products in stores today. Features 150 healthy recipes using convenience foods along with fresh fruits and vegetables. Explore creative ideas for old favorites, including Potato Salad, Stuffed Peppers, Quick Sloppy Joes, "Hot Dogs" and Beans, Lasagna, Chili, Bread Pudding, and Chocolate Pie. Menu ideas, food definitions, and product sources.

Available for $15. (208 pages)

Vegan Microwave Cookbook

Vegan Microwave Cookbook, by Nancy Berkoff, RD, offers over 165 recipes that can be prepared in a microwave oven. Many of the recipes will take under 10 minutes to cook. Others may be more appropriate for entertaining. Helpful advice includes: Converting Traditional Recipes to the Microwave, Microwave Baking and Desserts, Breakfast in a Snap, Curries and Casseroles, and Suggestions for Holidays and Parties. Sample dishes include Cilantro-Marinated Tofu, Basic "Meat" Balls, Microwave Lasagna, Pizza Potatoes, Coriander Kale with Slivered Carrots, Corn and Chili Muffins, and much more.

Available for $16.95. (288 pages)

Vegetarian Journal's Guide to Leather Alternatives

Besides not eating animals, you may not want to wear them! This guide is very helpful in locating non-leather items including shoes, belts, and bags. You'll even find sources for cruelty-free computer cases, Ipod and cell phone holders, skate boarding shoes, and much more. This comprehensive list includes store locations and online mail-order resources.

Available for $5. (8 pages)

Vegetarian Journal's Guide to Food Ingredients

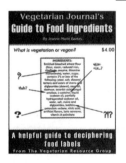

This guide is very helpful in deciphering ingredient labels. It lists the uses, sources, and definitions of hundreds of common food ingredients. The guide also states whether the ingredient is vegan, typically vegan, vegetarian, typically vegetarian, non-vegetarian, or typically non-vegetarian.

Available for $6. (28 pages)

Vegan Seafood

Vegan in Volume
Vegan Quantity Recipes for Every Occasion

Vegan in Volume, by Nancy Berkoff, RD, is a 272-page book. It has 125 quantity recipes for every occasion. Chef Nancy Berkoff offers help with catered events, weddings, birthdays, college food service, hospital meals, restaurants, dinner parties, etc. She shares her knowledge of vegan nutrition, vegan ingredients, menus for seniors, breakfast buffets, desserts, cooking for kids, and much more.

Available for $20. (272 pages)

Vegan Handbook

Vegan Handbook contains over 200 vegan recipes, including the basics, international cuisine, and gourmet dishes. Also features information on sports nutrition, a seniors' guide to good nutrition, feeding vegan kids, menus, guide to leather alternatives, vegetarian history, and much more. This is an 8-1/2 x 11-inch book!

Available for $20. (256 pages)

The Lowfat Jewish Vegetarian Cookbook

Jewish people throughout the world tradition-
ally have eaten healthy vegetarian meals. In
The Lowfat Jewish Vegetarian Cookbook, by
Debra Wasserman, you will find delicious
vegan recipes including Romanian Apricot
Dumplings, Fruit Kugel, Pumpernickel Bread,
Russian Flat Bread, Potato Knishes, Polish
Apple Blintzes, Indian Curry and Rice,
Hamentashen for Purim, and much more to
share with your family and friends. More than
150 lowfat international recipes are provided,
as well as breakfast, lunch, and dinner menus.
We've included nutritional analysis for each recipe. There are 33 dishes
suitable for Passover and Seder ideas, as well as Rosh Hashanah dinner
suggestions.

Available for $15. (224 pages)

No Cholesterol Passover Recipes

Featuring 100 Vegetarian Passover Dishes, *No
Cholesterol Passover Recipes*, by Debra Wasserman,
is a must for every home that wants to celebrate a
healthy and ethical Passover. Enjoy eggless blintzes,
dairy-free carrot cream soup, festive macaroons,
apple latkes, sweet and sour cabbage, knishes,
vegetarian chopped "liver," no-oil lemon dressing,
eggless matzo meal pancakes, and much more.

Available for $9. (96 pages)

Vegan Seafood

Vegan Passover Recipes

Vegan Passover Recipes, by Nancy Berkoff, EdD, RD, offers many eggless and dairy-free options for a healthy and great-tasting Festival of Freedom, including soups, salads, side dishes, sauces, entrées, and desserts. All recipes are suitable for Ashkenazi Eastern European Jewish tradition, which does not use beans or rice. Sample dishes include French Onion Soup, Pear and Apple Slaw, Minted Carrots with Chilies, Apricot and Tomato Sauce, Coconut Curry Over Greens, Spinach and Okra Stew, Moroccan Roasted Eggplant and Pepper Salad, Strawberry Sorbet, Cinnamon Matzah Balls, Pizza Casserole, Vegetarian Kishka, and much more.

Available for $6. (48 pages)

Vegan Menu for People with Diabetes

Chef Nancy Berkoff, EdD, RD, gives people with (or at risk for) diabetes a four-week meal plan, exchange listings for meat substitutes and soy products, and recipes for enjoyable dishes, such as Creamy Carrot Soup, Tangy Tofu Salad, Baked Bean Quesadillas, and French Toast.

Available for $10. (96 pages)

What is The Vegetarian Resource Group?

The Vegetarian Resource Group is a national non-profit organization that makes it easier to be vegetarian. Our registered dietitians, educators, and activists assist consumers, businesses, health professionals, and food services. Our public policy work is creating new opportunities for future generations of vegetarians.

◆ Publishers of *Simply Vegan, Meatless Meals for Working People, Vegan Meals for One or Two, Vegan in Volume, Vegan Menu for People with Diabetes, Vegan Passover Recipes, Vegetarian Journal,* and more.

◆ Online guide to vegetarian restaurants in the U.S.

◆ Fast food information

◆ Vegan recipes for individuals, families, and food services

◆ Vegetarian nutrition information that is both scientifically supported and practical

◆ Scholarships for high school seniors who actively promoted vegetarianism

◆ Sources for non-leather shoes, belts, coats, and other products

◆ Polls on the number of vegetarians

◆ Parents' e-mail list

◆ And much more…

The Vegetarian Resource Group

P.O. Box 1463, Baltimore, MD 21203

(410) 366-VEGE (8343); vrg@vrg.org

Don't forget to visit our website at www.vrg.org!